D0071670

Bible Studies for Special Occasions in Youth Ministry

Forrest W. Jackson,
Compiler/Contributor

B.J. Dean
Kathryn Griffin
Dan G. Kent
David Self
Vince Smith

BROADMAN PRESS
Nashville, Tennessee

Unless otherwise noted, all Scripture quotations are from the King James Version of the Bible.

Scripture quotations marked (NASB) are from the *New American Standard Bible*. Copyright © The Lockman Foundation, 1960, 1962, 1963, 1971, 1972, 1973, 1975. Used by permission.

Scripture quotations marked (NEB) are from the *New English Bible*. Copyright © The Delegates of the Oxford University Press and the Syndics of the Cambridge University Press, 1961, 1970. Reprinted by permission.

Scripture quotations marked (RSV) are from the Revised Standard Version of the Bible, copyrighted 1946, 1952, © 1971, 1973.

Scripture quotations marked (TEV) are from the *Good News Bible*, the Bible in Today's English Version. Old Testament: Copyright © American Bible Society 1976; New Testament: Copyright © American Bible Society 1966, 1971, 1976. Used by permission.

© *Copyright 1982* • *Broadman Press.*
All rights reserved.

4236-17
ISBN: 0-8054-3617-0

Dewey Decimal Classification: 220
Subject heading: BIBLE

Printed in the United States of America

Preface

The title of this book gives you the clue to its contents. This book contains twenty Bible studies for special occasions. These Bible studies can be used by any person who works with youth. They may be led by the Youth minister on the church staff or a lay leader whose responsibility is youth.

This unique book provides for those special times for youth when Bible study is an appropriate part. It is not planned for or to be in competition with any ongoing church activity or program.

The Bible studies involve twenty biblical personalities. They were chosen because their experiences parallel the developmental needs of youth. Some of these needs include decision making, accepting responsibility, witnessing, working, sibling relationships, loneliness, crisis experiences, dealing with feelings, God's call, and others. There are also studies that cover the special times of New Year's, Easter, and Fourth of July.

The writers of this book are all writers of Youth materials. They are people who know youth and their needs. They are people who know how to write to interest youth in Bible study. **B. J. Dean** is a homemaker in Mobile, Alabama. She teaches youth in her church. She is the author of *Teaching Youth in Sunday School*. **Kathryn ("Kitty") Griffin** is a pastor's wife in Lynchburg, Virginia. She works with and writes for youth. She is the author of *Teaching Teens the Truth* (Broadman). **Dan Kent** teaches the Old Testament at Southwestern Baptist Theological Seminary, Fort Worth, Texas. He is a frequent writer of Youth curriculum. He is the author of *Layman's Bible Book Commentary: Joshua, Judges, Ruth* (Broadman). **David Self** is minister of youth at First Southern Baptist Church, Del City, Oklahoma. He is the author of *Reaching Youth Through the Sunday School*. **Vince Smith** is pastor of South Garland Baptist Church, Garland, Texas. Prior to this he was Youth consultant in the Sunday School Division of the Baptist General Convention of Texas. He has written for numerous Youth periodicals. I am **Forrest W. Jackson**, editor of general religious books for Broadman Press. Prior to this assignment, I was design editor, Youth section, Sunday School Department, Baptist Sunday School Board.

As compiler, I have sought to bring some uniformity of method and approach to all of the Bible studies. At the same time, I have tried to allow the uniqueness of each writer to come through each study.

It is our hope that this book will truly be a meaningful part of your Youth ministry.

FORREST W. JACKSON

Contents

Absalom:

Destroyed by Hate

2 Samuel 13:1-39

Forrest W. Jackson

The Story of Lust (13:1-20)

This story begins like a modern-day novel. Amnon was David's firstborn son whose mother was Ahinoam. Amnon thought he was love sick (v. 2) over Tamar. She was the beautiful daughter of David and Maacah.

Since Tamar was a virgin daughter of King David, she had no way of meeting men. She was kept secluded in the palace. Even Amnon, heir to the throne, could not see her. Women like Tamar often led lonely existences because of the elaborate protection given to them by their fathers.

Amnon's friend, Jonadab, "the son of David's brother Shammah" (v. 3, TEV) suggested that Amnon play sick and ask David if Tamar could prepare a meal for him. Jonadab knew that David would let Amnon have whatever he wanted. Jonadab was right. Amnon went through his charade, and David sent Tamar to cook a meal for Amnon.

Amnon, however, was not hungry for food. His lust for Tamar had been allowed to get out of hand. He ran all his servants from his house and tried to get Tamar to have intercourse with him willingly.

Tamar quickly suggested that Amnon ask David if he could marry her. She also expressed the belief that David would let Amnon have his way (v. 13).

Evidently it was acceptable at this time for half brothers and sisters to be married. Abraham and Sarah were related in this way (Gen. 20:12). Amnon did not listen. Without regard for the anguished plea of Tamar, he pulled her into his bed and raped her. At this point the reader thinks, *finally it's over.*

But that was not the case. Having satisfied his lust, Amnon's so-called love turned to hate. He screamed at Tamar, "Get out" (v. 15). Could it be that looking at Tamar in her pitiful shape at that moment reminded him of his own perverseness and lack of self-control? Perhaps his hatred of Tamar was a self-hate. On the other hand perhaps he now saw her as soiled and unfit for the king-to-be. Such double standards still exist today. Young people often find that what they think will lead to ecstatic love actually leads to hate.

Tamar could not believe her ears. She must have said, "Amnon! You will marry me, won't you? Surely you won't take my virginity and then throw me out like a common prostitute!" (Tamar knew that a king's daugher who had lost her virginity had lost her usefulness to the royal family and her desirability to men seeking a wife of royalty.)

Amnon was beside himself as as he listened to Tamar's plea. He called for a servant to throw her out. Such was Amnon, heir to the throne of David.

Tamar tore the lovely robe with its long sleeves, as an act of deep grief. The special robe had marked her as a virgin daughter of David. Amnon's criminal act had robbed her of her most precious possession. She plodded despondently into the house of her full brother, Absalom.

Absalom knew at once what had happened (v. 20). He took Tamar into his own home and cared for her. The text indicates that Tamar may never have married. Perhaps she lived her life in sadness and loneliness in Absalom's house.

The Story of Inaction (13:21-22)

Absalom suggested to Tamar that the incident not be told. It would remain a family affair. No doubt Absalom expected David to punish Amnon, but it would remain a family affair. It would be kept from the public, so far as possible.

"When King David heard what had happened, he was furious" (v. 21). It would have been far better if he had disciplined Amnon. Evidently "furious" was all he could muster. There is no evidence that he even gave Amnon a tongue-lashing. Since this was an inter-family crime, David should have punished Amnon. However, David did nothing. Could it be that David's knowledge of his own sin with Bathsheba kept him from punishing Amnon? It would not be the first time, nor the last, that a father's own sinful life kept him from disciplining his children.

The biblical writer is silent as to David's reasons for not punishing Amnon. But Absalom was determined to get even with Amnon, if David failed. The law demanded that a man who raped an unengaged girl should pay her father fifty pieces of silver. Then he must marry her and "never divorce her as long as he lives" (Deut. 22:29).

The Story of Hate (13:22-29)

Absalom waited two years (v. 23), hating Amnon the entire time. He had decided to take matters into his own hands, since David had done nothing to Amnon.

Hate is like a hungry lion. Hate may look like an oversized kitten, but it's a lion that will eat you up. Everyone has had some experience that has brought hate into his life. Most call it dislike or something less than hate. Therein is the problem. Hate must be recognized and dealt with severely. If allowed to control one's life, hate is self-destructing.

Absalom hated Amnon for raping his sister. He hated his father for doing nothing to right the wrong done to Tamar. He hated Amnon to the point "that he would no longer even speak to him" (v. 22, TEV). Absalom wouldn't let it go. He nursed his hatred and kept it burning for two years.

Finally, Absalom's hatred moved him to action against his brother. He devised an elaborate plan to cover his real intention to murder Amnon. Absalom planned a festival party to coincide with the shearing of his sheep. This type of party was normal procedure for that day and didn't arouse the suspicions of David. Absalom did a lot of pleading to get David to come with his entire court (vv. 24-25). Absalom kept on until David was about to run him out of the palace. Then Absalom made his move. Perhaps under the guise of great disappointment Absalom said in effect, "Then let Amnon represent you and your court. I want my party to be recognized as *the* event of the year (v. 27*b*). Let Amnon represent your own presence."

David proved himself wishy-washy again. He first said no. But he finally gave in to Absalom's pleading. And by giving in to Absalom, David signed Amnon's death warrant. The entire project was one big cover-up of Absalom's determination to kill Amnon for raping his sister.

David had to share the blame for his wishy-washy and indulgent attitude toward the whole affair. But it was the grip of hatred upon Absalom that brought the hand of murder into the very family of David.

Absalom played the part of the gracious host to the nth degree. Everything was perfectly arranged. The food was magnificent and appealed to every taste bud around the table. The wine was the best in the kingdom. Absalom had calculated that Amnon would drink too much of the excellent wine (v. 28). Everything was perfect, including the signal from Absalom. The signal was given and Absalom's servants killed Amnon in one swift movement. Two years of hatred erupted in a moment of supposed family solidarity and joy. The hypocrisy had been carried out to the hilt of the assassin's knives. The heir to the throne of David was dead.

The Story of Broken Relationships (13:30-39)

The murder of Amnon moved the rest of David's sons to flight. Panic gripped their hearts as they probably thought Absalom planned to kill them all to get the throne himself. It had happened in other kingdoms and would yet happen in the dynasties of God's chosen people. Since Absalom didn't make a move toward anyone but Amnon, it seems likely that hatred, not the throne, was his motive at this time. Later, Absalom would make his move to take the throne from David.

The first news that reached David was that "Absalom has killed all your sons—not one of them is left!" (v. 30, TEV). However, Jonadab again showed his insight into personality. He said in effect, "Absalom only wanted to kill Amnon. It's been obvious since Amnon raped Tamar. The rest of your children are OK. You'll see."

The murder of Amnon cost Absalom three years of exile (v. 38). Hatred takes its toll. Either a person pays the price of getting rid of hatred, or he pays the higher price of the expression of hatred in his life.

Absalom's hatred evidently continued to control him. Hatred of David caused Absalom to seek to kill his father and to take the throne from him by force. Absalom couldn't wait for time to bring him the throne. Hatred burned and pushed him to take matters into his own hands. Ultimately, hatred caused his death.

Absalom had such promise. He was a very handsome and desirable young man. He had his father's ability to win the hearts of people. He knew how to lead. He had everything and one thing more, hatred. Hatred negated the positive elements. Hatred destroyed this promising young prince. Absalom was killed when the throne was practically in his grasp.

Here are some lessons we can learn from the life of Absalom:
1. Hatred is no respecter of persons.
2. Hatred is a destructive force.
3. Hatred focuses on pride and selfishness.
4. Hatred affects a person's reasoning ability.
5. Hatred leads to senseless acts of cruelty.
6. Hatred leads persons away from God's will.
7. Hatred destroys the hater.
8. Hatred is a sin against God.

SUGGESTIONS FOR LEADING THE BIBLE STUDY

From a study of the life of Absalom, youth can learn that hate is a destroyer of persons.

Get Ready

Prepare the questionnaire called for in step 1. Prepare the lectures for steps 2 and 4. Note that two different kinds of lectures are called for. Prepare the poster for step 5. Have pencils and paper ready. You could use the back of the questionnaire for notes in step 2.

Be sure that you are completely familiar with the story of Absalom. Read about Absalom in your Bible (2 Sam. 13—18). Read thoroughly the interpretation in this book. Ask the Holy Spirit to guide you to speak to the needs of youth through the life of Absalom.

Lead Bible Study

1. Ask the youth to find in their Bibles and read 2 Samuel 13:1-20. Then pass out copies of the questionnaire you prepared and ask the youth to fill it in, using the passage of Scripture they just read. Allow them to use their Bibles.

Questionnaire suggestions: (1) Who was Amnon? (2) Who was Tamar? (3) Why couldn't Amnon see Tamar? (4) Why do you think Amnon raped Tamar when he could have married her? (5) Why did Amnon's love for Tamar turn to hate (v. 15)?

Several of these are thought questions. Do not be afraid of differences of opinions. Help the youth to see the shallowness of Amnon's love, if it can be called love at all. He was selfish and thought only of himself. Youth also need to be aware that sexual intercourse in dating often leads to a kind of hatred, a turning away from and a despising of the person who has been used.

2. Using the material under the headings "The Story of Inaction (13:21-22)" and "The Story of Hate (13:22-29)," give a short lecture. Divide the youth into two listening groups. Give them pencils and paper. Ask one group to list the things David did. Ask the other group to list the things Absalom did. Be sure to bring out the fact that David did not discipline Amnon and left the door open for Absalom to plan his own revenge. Also bring out how Absalom nursed his hatred for two years. Point out how hatred consumes the hater.

Call for reports from the two teams. Fill in any gaps.

3. Lead in a discussion of how hatred destroys relationships. Ask, What are some ways that hatred enters into family relationships today? List them on the chalkboard or newsprint. Now ask, What form does hate usually take in Youth groups today? See if you can get some consensus on the question. Close the discussion by asking, What is the answer to this problem?

4. Ask the youth to read 2 Samuel 13:30-39 in their Bibles. When they have finished, ask them what price Absalom paid for his hatred.

From your reading of 2 Samuel 15:1-18; 18:6-18 and the material under the heading "The Story of Broken Relationships (13:30-39)," relate the end of Absalom's life and what hatred finally did to him. Absalom could not have become king without killing his father.

5. Show the poster containing the "lessons from the life of Absalom." (These "lessons" are found at the end of the biblical interpretation material.) Ask the youth to ignore the numbers. Have the youth pair off. Instruct them to decide which "lesson" speaks most clearly to them. Ask each person in each grouping to share how the statement applies to him. Ask them to have a prayer, asking God's help in dealing with hatred.

Barnabas:

The Ability to Encourage People

Acts 4:31-37; 9:26-30; 11:19-26; 13:13; 15:36-41

Forrest W. Jackson

Who was Joseph in the Book of Acts? Many youth know Joseph the patriarch in Genesis. More will know Joseph the husband of Mary. But, who is Joseph in the Book of Acts?

Because Joseph was a constant source of encouragement in the early church, the apostles called him Barnabas. The name means "Son of encouragement" (4:36, RSV). Youth might remember Barnabas as "Mr. Encouragement."

Barnabas proved himself to be an encourager in several ways. He sold his own property to pay for the needs of fellow Christians. He encouraged Gentiles who accepted Jesus by faith only. He accepted people like Saul of Tarsus who were friendless and hated and brought them into the church. And he gave people like John Mark a second chance to change failure into success.

Youth talk a lot about accepting people. However, in practice they are often cliquish and make it difficult for people to get into their group. People who need to learn the art of accepting and encouraging others can learn a great deal from Barnabas.

Barnabas Shared with Others (4:31-37)

The first time we meet Barnabas in Acts, he had sold a field and given the money to the apostles for the needy church members. There was no coercion. Some have sought to compare this sharing with present-day Communism. However, Communism is coercive and totalitarian. Christianity is not coercive. Christians give out of a spirit of love.

Barnabas gave because he wanted to give. He did it because he was a Christian and wanted to share with those less fortunate. Notice that Barnabas, and others, had been "filled with the Holy Spirit" (v. 31). This "filling" had led to the concrete act of giving that people might have their needs met. Barnabas' gift likely bought food for the very poor in the Jerusalem church.

The "filling" also resulted in a clear witness as they "spoke the word of

God with boldness" (v. 31, RSV). There was no tongue speaking. The message was clear, understandable, and bold.

Youth are often under the spell of acquiring things. They want cars, clothes, and money to do many things. Sometimes they are dependent upon parents for money. However, many youth today have enough money to meet their needs and beyond. Barnabas gives youth an example of unselfishness in giving, without external coercion.

Barnabas Accepted Saul (9:26-30)

Many youth have a close-knit group of friends. Even many youth who run with the gang have a closed group of friends. They often keep other youth out, especially youth they feel do not "fit."

Saul was the most unlikely candidate for Christianity imaginable. Only God would have thought of it. Saul would not have been on any Christian's soul-winning list. The reason was that you might be locked up in prison or killed before you had a chance to give your witness to Saul of Tarsus. The name *Saul* and the word *persecution* were synonymous to the early Christians.

This passage of Scripture doesn't tell us how Barnabas came to believe that Saul was truly converted. Perhaps Barnabas knew Ananias in Antioch and accepted his testimony. Perhaps the horror of the Jews that their number-one persecutor of the Christians had become converted convinced Barnabas. Perhaps Barnabas had a private meeting with Saul to determine for himself. However it happened, Barnabas was convinced that Saul was a Christian. And Barnabas didn't hold grudges. He accepted Saul because he was a Christian.

The Jerusalem church must have felt Saul was pulling a fast one, pretending to be a Christian. It would be a perfect ploy. Pretend to be a Christian, get into the church, get the names of the members, then call in the Sanhedrin's police and take the whole bunch to prison. Sounds like a spy story, doesn't it? And that's probably why "they were all afraid of him" (v. 26, TEV). You don't invite a spy inside and show him all your secrets. "They would not believe that he was a disciple" (v. 26, TEV).

The next words, "then Barnabas came to his help," (v. 27, TEV) indicate a new stance was about to be taken. Every church needs a Barnabas! Barnabas accepted people, even Saul. Barnabas gave people another chance. Barnabas was willing to stick his neck out for others. Barnabas encouraged those around him.

Barnabas must have had a private talk with Saul, for Barnabas knew the story of the Damascus-road experience (v. 27). He must have heard it from the lips of Saul. No doubt Barnabas was thrilled to see the power of Jesus at work in Saul. Jesus could take the church's worst enemy and make him the church's best friend.

Barnabas literally took his life in his hands in meeting Saul. He staked his life and the lives of others in the Jerusalem church on the fact that Saul was converted. Barnabas knew the power of Jesus to change lives. And Barnabas saw Jesus in Saul of Tarsus.

If the members of the Jerusalem church were afraid of Saul, they were convinced they could trust Barnabas. Because Barnabas said Saul was a Christian, Saul was accepted (v. 28).

Youth need people they can trust to lead them, people like Barnabas. And youth need to become people who are worthy of trust. Our world sorely needs leaders who can be trusted. Would someone in your community be able to become part of your Youth group if one respected youth would stand up for that person?

Everyone in Jerusalem must have been flabbergasted at Saul's "preaching boldly in the name of the Lord" (v. 28, TEV). Saul became a victim of his own former friends. Because of his effective preaching to "the Greek-speaking Jews" (v. 29, TEV), his life was threatened by his former friends. The Jerusalem Christians sent Saul "away to Tarsus" (v. 30, TEV) to save his life. Barnabas' care for Saul had multiplied. Now "the believers" (v. 30, TEV) were concerned for Saul, their new Christian brother.

Barnabas Asked Saul to Help Him (11:19-26)

Although the Jerusalem church was not as missionary oriented as Jesus had commanded, they did show good sense in sending Barnabas to check on the conversion of Gentiles in Antioch. Barnabas was open-minded and accepting of any person who believed in Jesus. When Barnabas arrived in Antioch "and saw the grace of God, he was glad; and he exhorted them all to remain faithful to the Lord with steadfast purpose" (v. 23, RSV). It was in his own joy at the Gentiles' conversion that Barnabas encouraged the new Christians. Barnabas believed Jesus could convert Gentiles, and he encouraged them all to be converted through faith in Jesus Christ.

What if the Jerusalem church had sent the narrow-minded Judaizers? What if the church had sent those who insisted that every Gentile must believe exactly like them before being accepted into the church? It could have been disastrous! However, the Holy Spirit caused the Jerusalem church to send Barnabas. His encouragement gave impetus to the great Antiochan evangelistic movement.

Also notice that Barnabas was "full of the Holy Spirit" (v. 24, TEV). Barnabas did not speak in tongues. Instead he "exhorted" (preached clearly and distinctly and understandably) them to be faithful to the Lord Jesus Christ (v. 23, RSV).

Barnabas found himself overwhelmed by the bold mission thrust of evangelism in Antioch. Many Gentiles had accepted Jesus before Barnabas came. Then in response to Barnabas' preaching, "many people were brought to the Lord" (v. 24, TEV). At this point the reader might expect Barnabas to do what any enterprising preacher or evangelist would do: hold a press conference with the media, prepare new brochures outlining the number of converts, plan new campaigns while the statistics are glowing.

But Barnabas wasn't a glory-seeker. Barnabas realized that the new converts were raw pagans. He knew they needed sound biblical instruction concerning the Christian life. "So Barnabas went to Tarsus to look for Saul; and when he had found him, he brought him to Antioch" (vv. 25-26, RSV). Without a doubt, Saul was a great interpreter of the Bible (Old Testament). His scholarship as a student of Gamaliel (see Acts 22:3) was turned to teaching the Christian gospel. Barnabas picked Saul because Saul had abilities he did not have. Barnabas picked his helper to complement his ministry. This is an example any pastor or administrator would do well to follow: call church staff members who complement each other.

A lesser man would not have sought a helper as strong as Saul. A lesser man would not want an equal or better. But Barnabas and Saul worked together for an entire year, following up that evangelistic thrust (v. 26b). They did their work so well, under the guidance of the Holy Spirit, that "the disciples were for the first time called Christians" (v. 26, RSV) right there in Antioch.

Youth often find themselves bombarded by competitiveness. Everywhere they turn it's compete, compete. In schoolwork, in sports, in music, in dating, in the family, competition is the name of the game. Who remembers the person who came in second? It is difficult for anyone to be gracious or to give someone better than oneself a chance to take first place. But Barnabas got the best, Saul. It was not long after this that Acts begins speaking of Saul and Barnabas rather than Barnabas and Saul. It is also about this time that Saul begins to be called Paul.

Barnabas Gave Mark a Second Chance (15:36-41)

On the first missionary journey of Barnabas and Paul (13:4 to 14:28), John Mark had gone with them "to assist them" (13:5). He may have instructed new converts while Barnabas and Saul preached the gospel. For some reason John Mark left the missionaries at "Perga in Pamphylia" (13:13, RSV).

In this same verse (13:13), Luke wrote, "Now Paul and his company." Could it be that Mark objected to Paul's taking over? Could it be that Mark was just too young to be as intense as Paul insisted? We will probably never know. One thing we do know. Paul thought Mark was a quitter (15:38), and Paul had no use for quitters.

When Paul suggested to Barnabas another missionary journey (v. 36), he was ready to go. Barnabas suggested that Mark should be given a second chance (v. 37) and go on the journey. However, Paul would not even consider the possibility (v. 38).

Barnabas, somewhat uncharacteristic of himself, must have argued long and loud on the side of giving Mark another chance. But Paul was adamant. The result was "a sharp contention, so that they separated from each other" (v. 39, RSV).

Barnabas paid a price to give Mark a second chance. "Barnabas took Mark with him and sailed away to Cyprus" (v. 39, RSV). Acts does not mention him again. Notice also that it was Paul and Silas that were "commended by the brethren to the grace of the Lord" (v. 40, RSV).

There are not many people who would turn down an opportunity to be on the winning team in order to give someone a second chance. Paul was obviously the winning team. But Barnabas believed in people more than in winning. Barnabas gave Mark a second chance. Youth need to learn this lesson. Youth know how desperately they long for a second chance. Yet they often will not go out of their way to offer another youth a second chance, when he desperately needs it. All of us need to learn from the example of Barnabas.

But consider what was gained by the attitude and action of Barnabas. (1) A Gospel writer was saved for Christian service. (2) Two missionary teams went out, instead of one. (3) Paul finally admitted that Barnabas was right in his estimation of Mark (see 2 Tim. 4:11).

Before youth think Barnabas was perfect and no one could follow him, they need to look at one instance where Barnabas was wrong. In Galatians 2:11-14, Paul told of Barnabas' joining Peter in discriminating against the Gentile Christians. They had done this because a group from the Jerusalem church had come to Antioch and would not eat with the Gentile Christians. Paul denounced both of them for "their cowardly action" (v. 13, TEV). Barnabas was not perfect, but he tried to follow Jesus with his whole heart. He was willing to pay the price to encourage the people of God.

Encouragement is greatly needed among youth today. The example of

Barnabas can guide the way. Youth need to be encouragers because: (1) Many youth are discouraged and feel that life has little to offer. Drugs become an escape from discouragement and an attempt to find courage. (2) Many youth find suicide to be a way out of their discouragement. (3) Their world is often negative and filled with put-downs. (4) Encouragement can become contagious. (5) God can use them to change his world for the better. (6) Youth have much to offer that their world needs.

SUGGESTIONS FOR LEADING THE BIBLE STUDY

From a study of the life of Barnabas, youth can learn how to be an encourager of others.

Get Ready

Read all of the passages in Acts in your Bible. Read the interpretation of this Scripture. If you have time, read several translations of each passage and a commentary, if you have one. Make the material your own. Get to know Barnabas personally.

Gather pencils and paper for steps 2 and 4. Have a 3-x-5 index card for each youth for step 5.

Lead Bible Study

1. Ask the youth if they know the nickname of Joseph in the Book of Acts. Give them a chance to recall the name of Barnabas. Use the opening paragraphs to give youth an introduction to Barnabas. Bring in the need of your youth to be encouraged in life. Speak to the fact that Barnabas got his new name because he was usually encouraging people. Get the idea across that youth can become good at encouraging others. Show that this study of Barnabas will give youth an idea of how to become encouragers.

2. Give the youth pencils and paper. Instruct them to turn to Acts 4:32-37 in their Bibles and read it. After they have read the Scripture, ask them to answer the following questions. (1) Why did Barnabas sell his field? (2) Why do you think Barnabas gave all he received for his field to the church? (3) How did this act of Barnabas encourage the church? (4) What does this Scripture passage teach you about encouragement?

When the youth have finished, ask them to share their answers. Don't spend too much time but allow each question to be answered by a youth. Add your comments where necessary.

3. Ask the youth to read Acts 9:26-30. Ask them what kind of person Saul of Tarsus was. Then ask, Would you have witnessed to a person like Saul? Finally, What kind of person would Saul be today? Help them to think of

someone they might run into in their community.

Using the material under the heading "Barnabas Accepted Saul (9:26-30)," recount the story of Barnabas helping Saul to be accepted by the Jerusalem church. Be sure to show that Barnabas had to take a risk to include Saul in his group.

Ask your youth, How can you encourage a youth who is outside your group? What risks would be involved?

4. Divide the youth into four groups. If your group is large, double the number. Give two groups the same assignment. Each group will read Acts 11:19-26. Provide pencils and paper. Group 1: What part did the Jerusalem church play in this passage? (They might suggest: sent Barnabas to check Antioch, expected a report, not personally involved.) Group 2: What part did Barnabas play in this passage? (They might suggest: was glad about Gentile conversion, accepted Gentile Christians, preached the gospel, went to get Saul.) Group 3: What part did Saul play in this passage? (They might suggest: went to help Barnabas, taught for a year.) Group 4: What can youth do today to encourage others like Barnabas encouraged the people at Antioch? (They might suggest: establishing friendship with a new Christian in their church.) Give youth about ten minutes and call for reports.

5. Read Acts 15:36-41 aloud while the youth follow in their Bibles. Ask a youth to read Acts 13:4-5,13. Be sure the youth understand that Mark was a part of the missionary team of Barnabas and Saul, but he left them. No one knows why.

Ask, Would you want to give Mark a second chance by asking him to go on the next missionary journey you took? Why? Why not?

Remind them that Barnabas got into a heated argument with Paul over Mark. In fact, they broke off their association. Use the material under "Barnabas Gave Mark a Second Chance (15:36-41)" to fill in the story.

Ask the youth to take a moment to think of someone they know who needs a second chance. Ask them to decide how they will give this person a second chance. Give each youth a 3-x-5 index card and a pencil. Ask them to write on the card: "I will give (person's name) a second chance this week." Suggest that they put the card in their Bibles as a reminder.

Close with prayer, asking God to challenge the youth to become encouragers of others.

Daniel:

The Courage of Convictions
Daniel 1:1-17; 2:1-24; 6:1-23; 12:1-3

Kathryn Griffin

Daniel was a prisoner in a distant land. It's not easy to be a prisoner. We often forget that fact. It's not easy to adjust to a foreign country when we've been taken there against our will. It's not easy to accept what we cannot change. It's not easy to brighten the corner where we are if we don't want to be in that corner in the first place. We know, from his own account, that Daniel never forgot his homeland and the way things used to be. When we consider the many excuses he could have had for being an angry, resentful, brooding young man, Daniel is all the more remarkable for the things he allowed God to do in his life.

> The king ordered Ashpenaz, his chief official, to select from among the Israelite exiles some young men of the royal family and of the noble families. They had to be handsome, intelligent, well-trained, quick to learn, and free from physical defects, so that they would be qualified to serve in the royal court. Ashpenaz was to teach them to read and write the Babylonian language (Dan. 1:3-4, TEV).

The Cream of the Crop

When King Nebuchadnezzar of Babylonia defeated Jerusalem, Daniel was one of the prisoners taken back to Babylonia. Because he was handsome, intelligent, well trained, disciplined, and had a royal background, Daniel was one of the ones chosen for special training in his new land. He was to be given a special education and groomed for leadership in the Babylonian government.

There are several ways that Daniel and his friends could have reacted to this turn of events. They could have sulked and rebelled against their captors and refused to have anything to do with them. On the other hand, they could have identified with their captors to the extent that they completely turned their backs on their own people and ways and teachings. Or they could have been two-faced. They could have pretended to cooperate fully with the Babylonians while all the time plotting ways and means of getting even or of staging a revolt.

The selected young men did none of those things. They accepted the opportunity for an education and for the leadership positions that would be theirs, if selected by the king. They seemed to have a keen understanding of the fact that God can make it possible for good to come out of evil.

But Daniel purposed in his heart that he would not defile himself with the portion of the king's meat, nor with the wine which he drank" (1:8).

Being Different

Everybody else was doing it. Eating meat and drinking wine was the "in" thing at the Babylonian court. In fact, the king had ordered that the Hebrew youths be as well fed as other members of the court.

But Daniel was concerned. The religious laws he had been taught all his life forbade the eating of meat (or at least the kind he was being required to eat). He knew that the drinking of wine was not in his best interests. He had a problem.

Daniel could have reasoned that to say something about his diet was running a risk. He could offend the king. He might be laughed at by other members of the court. He could be ridiculed and subsequently mistreated by the officials in charge of his training. He might even be dropped from the training program. He could run the risk of having his own friends and countrymen fail to take the same stand he wanted to take. Maybe he should just be quiet and give it a try, he could have reasoned. Maybe the food wouldn't hurt him. Maybe his childhood teachings were all wrong. After all, when in Babylonia shouldn't one do as the Babylonians were doing?

Daniel didn't take the easy way out. He made up his mind to be true to his beliefs. He would not turn his back on his God. He would stand alone if necessary. He would show respect for his body. He would take the risks.

After Daniel made his decision concerning the kind of food he would like to eat, he handled his decision in an admirable way. Instead of belligerently announcing his intentions, he asked permission of the authorities to give his diet a ten-day trial. His request was granted, and the experiment worked.

Courtesy and consideration for the rights and feelings of others works wonders. Taking a stand for one's Christian convictions earns the respect of other people. Putting Christian beliefs into action produces growth and further commitment.

He told them to pray to the God of heaven for mercy and to ask him to explain the mystery to them (2:18, TEV).

The Value of Prayer

King Nebuchadnezzar had a frightening dream one night. None of his fortunetellers or magicians could interpret the dream, primarily because the king couldn't even remember what he had dreamed! He just remembered that it was an important dream. The king threatened to put to death all his advisers, including Daniel and his friends.

Daniel requested and received time to work on the matter. He and his friends prayed earnestly for understanding and for the key to the mystery of the dream. That night the mystery was revealed to Daniel. Immediately thereafter, he remembered to praise and thank God for his obvious intervention. In a song of praise, Daniel said, "He controls the times and the seasons;/ he makes and unmakes kings;/ it is he who gives wisdom and understanding" (2:21, TEV).

All too often, prayer is the resource we use last in seeking understanding. Wisdom and insight are gifts from God, but he is eager to bestow them on anybody who is interested in having them. The more we pray, the more God teaches us about himself. The more God teaches us about himself, the more we understand about people and incidents around us. The better we get to know God, the more confident we become as we take stands in his behalf.

> God sent his angel to shut the mouths of the lions so that they would not hurt me (6:22, TEV).

Facing the Lions

Daniel was appointed by King Darius to be the first of 3 presidents over 120 princes who would help rule the country. The governors and officials under Daniel's supervision were jealous of him and devised a scheme for getting rid of him. They suggested to the king that he make a law forbidding anyone to seek advice or ask for help from anybody but the king for thirty days.

King Darius was very pleased! He thought the law was a good idea. He had no idea what was about to happen.

Daniel learned of the order, but still he continued to kneel and pray to his God, as always. His enemies knew that he would do that and after observing him at prayer, they reported him to the king.

The king had been tricked! Sadly, he sentenced Daniel to the lions' den and then embarked on one of the most miserable nights of his entire existence.

But Daniel survived the night, as he felt sure he would. At dawn when the king came to the pit to check on his favorite assistant, Daniel was able to call out to him. God "did this because he knew that I was innocent and because I have not wronged you, Your Majesty," Daniel said.

Most Christians feel that they sometimes have to face the lions on Christ's behalf. In countries where citizens do not experience the kind of religious freedom we take so lightly and so for granted, the lions might take the form of imprisonment, censorship, constant harassment, banishment, and even death. In countries where religious freedom is a constant reality, the lions may take the form of ridicule, misunderstanding, inadequate wages and compensations, the need to deny self and the relinquishing of possible material gains and comforts, as well as the accusations of our own consciences.

All the people of your nation whose names are written in God's book will be saved (12:1, TEV).

Good Will Triumph Over Evil

Through a series of visions and symbols, Daniel explained to his countrymen that hard times were ahead of them. Not only would they be repressed by political and military leaders and lose their freedom and many of their human rights, but "The Awful Horror" would be placed on the Temple. God's people will not be allowed to offer sacrifices and offerings and worship in his house.

We who are oversaturated with church activities might tend to underestimate what an "Awful Horror" it would be to be deprived of our church buildings. The sharing of our faith is a more valuable privilege than we realize. To be cut off from other Christians and to be prevented from worshiping, learning, praising, and fellowshiping in our usual group settings would leave us with enormous vacuums in our lives. The props we provide each other's lives would be knocked out from under us.

But God assures us that right will triumph over wrong. He has provided salvation from forces both without and within which would seek to destroy us. In spite of the blackest, bleakest of days when evil seems sure to win out, the Christian can be assured that ultimately, "The wise leaders will shine with all the brightness of the sky. And those who have taught many people to do what is right will shine like the stars forever" (12:3, TEV).

God does not promise that he will provide victory in the exact manner in which we may be expecting it. He will provide it in the way that will be best for us here on earth. (Virtue is sometimes its own reward.) Then heaven will be far better than we can visualize with the kinds of minds that we have to work with while we are human beings.

SUGGESTIONS FOR LEADING THE BIBLE STUDY

From a study of the life of Daniel, youth can learn the courage to live by their convictions.

Get Ready

Prepare copies of the questionnaire to be used under 1. Study carefully the story of Daniel. Be prepared for any lecture you plan to use.

Lead Bible Study

1. Create interest in the study of Daniel and his courageous stands for God by distributing copies of the following questionnaire and allowing about fifteen minutes for the completing of the unfinished statements and the sharing of opinions.

(1) When I am called on to take a stand that's based on my religious convictions, it's usually in the area of _____ or _____. (2) The last time I was in the minority in regard to a moral issue, I . . . (3) Youth must often make ethical and moral decisions concerning _____, _____, _____, _____, and _____. (4) The one situation that causes the most youth to abandon their religious training is . . . (5) The area in which I have the most trouble being true to my religious convictions is . . . (6) The area in which I have the least trouble being true to my religious convictions is . . . (7) I could do a whole lot toward strengthening my religious convictions by . . .

2. Assign the following Scripture passages to various individuals or teams of youth and instruct the youth to summarize the incident described: Daniel 1:1-7; 1:8-17; 2:1-13; 2:14-24; 6:1-13; 6:14-23; 12:1-3. Review important points in the story of Daniel's life by calling for answers to these questions: (1) How did Daniel happen to be in Babylonia? (2) How do we know that Daniel was an outstanding young man? (3) What can we learn from Daniel regarding a person's response to captivity? (4) What can we learn from Daniel's handling of the matter of his diet? (5) What special skill/skills did Daniel possess? How did he use them to bring honor to his God? (6) Pretend you are Daniel and explain your feelings about prayer. (7) What does Daniel's honesty with King Nebuchadnezzar in regard to his dream teach us about witnessing and about the special responsibilities of technical advisers and consultants? (8) Suggest some reasons why Daniel's witnessing methods were well accepted by some of the Babylonians and rejected by others. (9) Explain how the governors under Daniel's supervision tricked King Darius into sentencing Daniel to the lion's den. (10) Name difficulties, obstacles, pressures, and temptations faced by contemporary Christians that could be considered symbolic of the lion's den that Daniel faced. (11) Name at least three religious convictions to which Daniel remained true throughout his life. (12) Name three religious convictions to which you remain true most of the time. Be sure that you can answer these questions. Be prepared to add to the youth's answers. (Alternate: Lecture on this material. Give each youth a copy of the review

questions. Ask them to listen for the answers while you lecture. Call for reports.)

3. Lead youth to see the overriding truths in the study of Daniel by making these assignments to individuals or teams: (1) Name ways other than military in which the human body and mind may be held captive. (2) Describe a disappointing circumstance which might prove to be an opportunity for training, growth, and/or service. (3) List ways in which youth may, by their example, lead and influence others not to defile their bodies. (4) Formulate a set of commandments (thou shalt's and thou shalt not's) regarding the matter of being different from the crowd. (When should you? When should you not? How can you influence without offending? Must one never offend another?) (5) List at least five areas of contemporary life in which wrong seems to triumph repeatedly over right. Find a Scripture verse in Daniel which offers advice concerning the matter.

David:

Use Your Ability

1 Samuel 17

Vince Smith

The greatest king to ever rule Israel was David, the young shepherd, chosen by God and anointed by the prophet Samuel. David had an openness and willingness to follow God's leadership, a commitment often lacking in persons twice his age.

David's life is chronicled in the Old Testament between 1 Samuel 16 and 2 Kings 2, with much of the material paralleled in 1 Chronicles 2—29. He was of the tribe of Judah and became the second king of Israel. David served as forerunner and foreshadower of the Lord Jesus Christ. A great-grandson of Ruth and Boaz, David was the youngest of Jesse's eight sons. He was reared to be a shepherd. David incurred the wrath, jealousy, and ill will of his older brothers to a great extent because of the God-endowed talents he possessed. He is the only man in the Scriptures called "the man after God's own heart" (1 Sam. 13:14).

David's deep spiritual insights and intense feeling for God are reflected in the multitude of songs he wrote. David's ability as a musician is underscored by the obviously God-inspired psalms he penned. The body of David's music, when collected, became part of the Book of Psalms, a basic worship resource in every generation since the days of corporate worship in Solomon's Temple.

The Bible does not gloss over David's sins or character defects. The sin of David in the matter of the Hittite Uriah and his wife Bath-sheba illustrates this fact. But, David's moral blot was a stain on a character that was otherwise honest and sensitive to the voice of God. How wonderful it is to realize that God does not abandon his children when they fail. Instead, he is ready, willing, and able to pick them up, bless their lives, and once again make their lives blessings to others.

A Definition of Terms

Talents and *gifts* are words that need defining for most Christians. Some people see these words as interchangeable in meaning. In actuality, their meanings are unique and distinct. Webster defines a talent as a person's natural endowment or a characteristic feature, aptitude, or disposition. Talents may be influenced by one's genes and/or environment. Talents are reflected in musical ability, athletic prowess, and academic achievement. A talent may be cultivated and enhanced through continued use and efforts at development. Everyone has talents—even if a person seeks to deny them, ignore them, or fail to develop them. No one is talentless. A problem often arises over the fact that many individuals, rather than enhancing their natural talents, deny them and seek to be what they are not.

Spiritual gifts are not the same as talents. Gifts are abilities that God the Holy Spirit gives to believers at the time of conversion for the building up of the body of Christ, the church. The apostle Paul suggested that the gifts of the Spirit are special endowments given to members of the church for its service. The church is to be a community under the direction of the Holy Spirit. The special endowments are given at the discretion of the Holy Spirit. And, as gifts, they are not to be sought or asked for, but simply received and utilized in the ministry of Christian service.

Although spiritual gifts describe New Testament endowments upon believers, God gave Old Testament individuals, like David, special spiritual endowments in particular instances to enable those people to accomplish God's divine will. Talents, abilities, and spiritual gifts can today be used to build God's kingdom, strengthen his community of faith, accomplish his will in specific instances, and lead others to acknowledge the ultimate power and authority of God.

Samuel Anoints David King

First Samuel 16 records Samuel's anointing of David. This chapter reveals David's power as being the presence of the Holy Spirit upon his life (see 16:13). It is apparent that for anyone to effectively utilize his talents or spiritual endowments he must do so to accomplish God's will. David was a man who continually sought the will of God in all areas of life—even when he was being pursued vehemently by Saul. On several occasions, David had the opportunity to take Saul's life. But he chose not to do so because he realized that act would be outside of God's will (see 1 Sam. 26:9-11). Even though God had directed Samuel to anoint David and David's leadership was unquestioned by hundreds of people, God's will for David was to wait upon the Lord. Often we fail to realize that talents and abilities can enable us to more perfectly follow God's will.

Someone once said, "I don't want to give my life to be a foreign missionary, for just as soon as I do he will send me to Africa, and I don't want to go there!" That comment expresses a significantly warped view of God and his will for an individual's life. First, God does not want persons to go for him under coercion. Second, God's will is not to be visualized as a judge issuing sentences of condemnation. Third, God's will is not "castor oil"; it is "honey."

David came to realize that for many years God had been preparing him to become king. God's will involved a daily submissiveness, a daily willingness on the part of David. Rather than complaining about having to care for his father's sheep all alone in an isolated wilderness, David used the opportunity to acquire skills and sharpen talents and abilities endowed by God.

Seeking and following God's will today ensures that one is moving in the direction of God's ultimate will. A five-year-old illustrated this truth most ably. The young boy was playing with Lego blocks. These small, domino-size, plastic pieces snap together, enabling the child to be a builder of "anything." The Lego blocks illustrate God's will in one's life. As talents and abilities are dedicated to God and his service, God daily fits the pieces of our lives together. Ultimately, the products will be finished, but today we must be satisfied with knowing that our lives have been lived in the center of God's will to the best of our abilities. And one must be satisfied in knowing that daily walking in God's will results in God's best for an individual (see Phil. 2:13).

Avoid Wrong Use of Abilities

Just as talents and abilities can be dedicated to God, they may also be used for wrong and ultimately bring God's wrath and corrective hand upon an individual. David learned this lesson in the most difficult of ways. King David was immensely respected by his people. God had endowed him with the power to build a fortified nation. His natural ability to lead had been abundantly blessed by God. King David had only to make a request and it would be met. But, on a particular evening, the gifted king used his ability to lead in a manner inconsistent with God's will. The result was isolation from God; the death of Uriah; adultery with Bathsheba, the wife of Uriah; and the death of the child conceived in adultery. Ultimately, scores of people were affected simply because King David chose to use a God-given ability in opposition to God's will. This resulted in God's wrath upon David.

Sin is always punitive. The damage must be paid for. No one, not even King David, gets by without experiencing the consequences of the sins committed. The experience of David should be a reminder that a life committed to God can be wrongly swayed if the individual fails to constantly and continually seek to discern and follow God's divine will.

Allow God to Use You for Good

David's abilities and gifts were used by God in a remarkable manner to bring about good for the lives of others. David's encounter with Goliath,

David's serving of King Saul, and David's establishing a united Israel illustrate God's remarkable ability to empower David to accomplish tremendous feats that resulted in both blessing for David and glory to God.

When David encountered Goliath (see 1 Sam. 17), Saul's army was cowering at the brashness of an ungodly Philistine. David's arrival in the camp was little noticed. But, his confidence in God and total dependence upon the presence of God in the situation, resulted in a great Hebrew victory. Ultimately, God was able to demonstrate not only his power but his remarkable love for his people also.

Today, the same God who guided that stone flung from David's sling desires to give direction to the lives of all believers. But often believers are oppressed by the circumstantial giants that they encounter, failing to realize and acknowledge the power of the God of creation that is available to them. Christians today must act in faith, as did David. A responsive, dependent faith is necessary. But faith must be actualized, allowing God to control and direct the talents and gifts bestowed upon each individual believer.

In serving Saul (see 1 Sam. 18:5), David demonstrated his willingness to be faithful even when he was not in the spotlight or when he was putting to use a gift that was less spectacular than the confidence in God demonstrated when he brought Goliath to the ground. The behind-the-scenes persuasive spirit of David allowed him to unite twelve previously loosely connected tribes in a cohesive, God-sensitive spirit of common commitment.

Talents, gifts, and abilities can be used to accomplish significant feats for God or they can lie undeveloped and finally atrophy. The decision rests upon the individual. David illustrates the life of one continually open to allowing the power of God to activate and infuse the talents, gifts, and abilities he had placed at David's disposal.

SUGGESTIONS FOR LEADING THE BIBLE STUDY

From a study of the life of David, youth can learn that God's gift of talents and spiritual gifts should be used to do God's will.

Get Ready

Prepare the lecture for step 1. You will need a half-sheet of paper and a pencil for each youth for steps 2 and 3. You will need the use of a chalkboard and chalk or some other means of writing for steps 3 and 4. Several steps call for you to lead a discussion. You will need to be familiar with the Scripture lesson and the background material.

Lead Bible Study

1. Prepare a lecture to present an overview of David's life. Be sure to give

only the highlights. Be brief. Emphasize the talents and spiritual gifts of David.

2. Ask, What is the difference between talents and spiritual gifts? Use the discussion in this session to help youth understand the difference. Point out that no one is "talentless" or "giftless."

Give each youth a half-sheet of paper and a pencil. Instruct the youth to list their talents or abilities on their paper. When they have completed their list, instruct them to circle those talents/abilities they are willing to dedicate to God and to use in their daily living to bring honor to their Lord, Jesus Christ. Lead in a dedicatory prayer.

3. Ask the youth to turn to 1 Samuel 17 in their Bibles and to read the chapter. Give the youth another half-sheet of paper. Ask them to list "good" excuses David could have made to keep from confronting Goliath. When they have finished, list the excuses on the chalkboard or on newsprint. Ask, Do present-day Christians often make the same excuses when confronted with barriers in life as significant as Goliath was to the Hebrew army? Then ask, How can we receive God's help to use the abilities and gifts he has given us? (Youth can pray, do God's will as they know it, and learn to use well what God has given them.)

4. On a chalkboard (newsprint or butcher paper) begin to list the talents and abilities David possessed. Ask the youth to add their thoughts to the list. After the list has been completed, point out that even though David was a wise, able, and competent leader he was not perfect. In fact, the result of his misuse of power affected countless lives. Share with the youth a brief overview of the sad events surrounding David's adulterous relationship with Bathsheba (see 2 Sam. 11:1 to 12:25). Help the youth see that when their talents and abilities are misused God may have to discipline and punish them, just as he had to deal with David. Lead the youth to see that talents and abilities are given by God to be used to bring glory and honor to his name. Close with prayer being said silently by each youth. Ask them to silently recommit their lives, talents, and abilities to the service of the Lord and Savior, Jesus Christ.

Elijah:

How to Deal with Your Feelings
1 Kings 18:17-45; 19:9-18

B. J. Dean

Teenagers are not the only ones who experience quick mood changes. Elijah, the great prophet of God, one of those chosen to appear with the Christ at his transfiguration, was a man of many moods. The great fluctuation of feelings may have been a contributing factor in Elijah's failure to face a spiritual reality. His thinking had become clouded. These are not unique weaknesses; most of us suffer from the same problems.

Without introduction and with no hint of preparation for his coming one day, the prophet Elijah appeared in the court of Ahab, king of Israel. This prophet announced that a terrible drought would come to all the land and last until he gave the word that the situation was going to change (1 Kings 17:1). This was a judgment against the sins of the people of Israel. Then Elijah disappeared.

That was pretty impressive. The first of the major prophets and the most important leader of the worship of God since Moses and Samuel did not waste time with his credentials. He simply identified himself as a servant of the living God, made his statement, and disappeared for three years from Israel. It didn't rain. That was not only impressive in Israel but it was also disastrous! But for the God who had sent the drought, taking care of Elijah during this time was a small effort.

Three long, dry years passed. Don't you wonder about all the feelings the prophet must have had to deal with during those long days? Over a thousand of them! Then God told Elijah to go back to Israel and to Ahab and show the people that he was God—not Baal or any of the other false gods Queen Jezebel was influencing the people to worship.

The Contest (1 Kings 18:17-39)

One of the most exciting and dramatic events in the Bible took place when Elijah set out to prove to Israel who was the one, true God.

Elijah left the safety of his waiting place with a sense of security. Now that seems a bit hard to believe. Ahab and Jezebel had killed most of the prophets and priests of Jehovah and had diligently searched for Elijah to kill him. God told Elijah to walk bravely back into Israel and confront Ahab. Elijah did.

Ahab was the most perverse king ever to sit on the throne of Israel. He seemed to be addicted to doing evil. What kind of wife would a man like that want? Right! One who would share or even add to his life-style. That was Jezebel. Even her name has come to symbolize wickedness and treachery. What a pair! And they were on the throne of the nation of God's chosen people. Such an arrangement could not continue indefinitely. The day of reckoning had to come. It did.

Elijah and Ahab met. Immediately Ahab verbally attacked the prophet. Imagine the fury the king must have released! He had seen this man only one other time—three-and-a-half years earlier. At that time the prophet had boldly announced that God was alive, that the prophet stood before God, and that a drought would come. Now Elijah and Ahab were again face-to-face. Ahab was furious. He hurled this abuse at the prophet: You are the one causing all this trouble! You are responsible for this horrible drought! You are responsible for this famine we are suffering!

How typical of the truly evil person! Ahab would assume no personal responsibility for what had happened. It was always someone else's fault.

Elijah did not flinch at the king's fury. He was there at God's command, and he was confident of his position. He looked Ahab in the eye and bravely retorted, "Not I, Ahab. You. You and your family have chosen deliberately to forsake the laws of God to follow the falseness of Baal." Then he issued his challenge. Ahab offered no defense. Elijah had exposed the wickedness of the king. Ahab's only recourse was to accept the challenge and hope (don't you wonder if he really did) that Baal would win!

Let's look at that challenge (v. 19). The event was to take place on Mount Carmel. This was one of the most favored and fruitful spots in the whole of Palestine. It overlooked the blue Mediterranean Sea, so it enjoyed the breezes and mist of the sea. It was a fertile place where crops grew to perfection. Ahab probably thought that here the prophets of Baal could surely demonstrate the power of the god of fruitfulness and fertility. Isn't that strange? The king and queen encouraged the worship of such a god, so why had they not asked him to relieve the drought conditions before now?!

The participants were to be Elijah on God's side and 850 prophets on the side of Baal and Asherah. Those were not really terrific odds.

So the prophets met. The people of Israel gathered for the contest. After all, in this time of terrible drought there was not a lot to do anyway. This would help to pass another hot, dry day. Elijah was not going to let the people just watch however. Immediately he challenged them, "How long are you going to sit on the fence between two loyalties? Go one way or the other! Give your full allegiance to God or to Baal—but stand for something!" Think back. For almost six hundred years this nation had vacillated in their allegiance to God. He had barely gotten them out of Egypt before they became divided in their loyalties. This kind of conduct had gone on and on in spite of the judges, prophets, and priests God had sent to them. The people were still at it. Again a prophet said to them: Choose!

Then Elijah revealed that he thought he was alone in the worship of God. He wasn't, but at this time he was the only one acting as a prophet! He was standing against 450 prophets of Baal. (Apparently the four hundred prophets of Asherah had not accepted the challenge—which says something about their confidence in their god!) Elijah gave the challenge. He asked for two bullocks—one for him and one for the prophets of Baal. These animals were to be prepared and placed on the altar with everything ready for the sacrifice—except the fire. The true God or Baal would be called upon to provide the fire. The people loved it! It was going to be an exciting day!

Do you remember the importance of the offering of a bull? Look at Leviticus 16:6. A bull was a priest's offering for his own sin and wrongdoing. God himself had instituted this offering for his spiritual leaders, recognizing that his prophets and priests needed preparation of spirit, soul, and body to accomplish his will and work. The prophets of Baal did not recognize their spiritual needs; the servant of God still recognized his own unworthiness. He was giving honor to God, and God honors those who honor him.

Elijah generously told the prophets of Baal that they could go first. He gave his opponents every possible advantage. They performed their rituals. Nothing happened. By noon Elijah was mocking them. Actually he was doing more than enjoying some sarcasm. He was using every resource he could to combat a false religion. He told the prophets of Baal to keep trying. They did. They became more frenzied in their pleas to Baal—even to the point of self-laceration. Still nothing happened.

The day had been long, but finally it was Elijah's turn. Truth was about to have its hour. Elijah prepared his altar with twelve stones for the tribes of Israel. Around this, he dug a trench and put the prepared bull on the altar with the wood. Then he doused all of this with enough water even to fill the trench. (This water must have seemed very precious after a three-year drought!) After his preparations were completed, Elijah appealed to God in a simple, quiet, dignified prayer. God answered with fire (lightning, perhaps) from heaven that not only burnt the offering but also the wood, the stones, the dust, and even consumed the water. That was certainly an impressive demonstration—one that the people could not ignore. They didn't. (See v. 39.)

Those odds may not have been quite what they seemed; 450 *versus* Elijah plus God was more accurate. One plus God is always enough!

A Pinnacle of Faith (1 Kings 18:40-45)

After the destruction of Baal's prophets, Elijah told Ahab to get down from the mountain or he'd be caught by the rain. Rain? It was a cloudless day. Elijah went to the top of Mount Carmel where he could look out to the sea. He prayed while his servant watched. Finally the report came that there was a tiny cloud about the size of a man's hand rising from the sea. Remember even before this tiny cloud had appeared, Elijah had said, "There is a sound of abundance of rain" (v. 41). God had said the drought would end. Elijah believed him.

From the Pinnacle to the Pits—Read 1 Kings 19:9-18

What an experience Elijah had just had! However, he had killed the priests of Baal, and Jezebel was out to get him! Elijah fled to Horeb (Mount Sinai), a very holy place for the Jews. There he despaired (v. 10). God wanted to get Elijah's attention. He sent a great wind, an earthquake, and a fire— natural forces that traditionally were signs of God's presence. This time God was not in them. But he was there—in a still, small voice that asked again, "What are you doing here, Elijah?" (vv. 9,13, RSV).

With his face covered, Elijah repeated his plight (v. 14). This time God gave Elijah some tasks to perform. There was no time for self-pity. God's work is going to go on. The question each must ask is, Will it go on with my help or without it? God had allowed Elijah a short time to be depressed. That was acceptable, but it could not become a way of life. He told Elijah to look at one fact (v. 18). Elijah was not the only one left worshiping God! He had seven thousand others who shared his faith. What did Elijah do? He did what God told him to! That's always a good way to fight depression.

And So . . .

From Elijah we can learn that (1) it pays to be faithful to God even when you think you are standing alone; (2) periods of depression often follow great spiritual victories; and (3) depression can be overcome by getting busy and doing the will of God.

SUGGESTIONS FOR LEADING THE BIBLE STUDY

Through a study of the life of Elijah, youth discover the ways God helped Elijah in his times of joy and depression and how those ways are adaptable to the lives of youth today.

Get Ready

Prepare a focal wall with large, colorful letters that spell out: ELIJAH: How to Deal with Your Feelings.

Label a large strip of butcher paper in the following manner.

THE CONTEST

The Place   The Participants   The Preparation   The Prayer   The Results

Put the "And So" statements on a sheet of newsprint for use in step 4. Provide a pencil and paper for each person.

Lead Bible Study

1. Enlist two young men to sit on either side of a small table at the front of the room and give a demonstration of an arm wrestling contest. Encourage the group to give vocal support to the wrestler of their choice. After the contest is over, ask the youth what a contest is, what a contest proves, and how lasting the results of most contests are.

Explain that in the contest between Elijah and prophets of Baal one participant—the winner—was a man of many moods and how the contest excitement quickly changed to depression.

2. Request the group to open their Bibles to 1 Kings 17:1. Give a short lecture on the situation that existed in Israel at this time, the characteristics of Ahab and Jezebel. Examine the message in the suggested verse. Then point out that seemingly out of nowhere Elijah appeared, gave his message and disappeared again for about three-and-a-half years. Comment that although you will not deal with the events that took place during that time, it is pertinent for the group to express some of the feelings they think Elijah may have experienced during this time. (Some of these may have been fear, anxiety, frustration, impatience, apprehension, etc.)

3. Indicate the sheet of butcher paper on the focal wall and assign each column to a different team to listen for information to put on the chart as you read aloud 1 Kings 18:17-39. Complete the chart and allow the youth to share in the discussion/lecture that presents the dramatic event.

Select a youth to read aloud 1 Kings 18:41-45 and ask the youth to identify the evidences of Elijah's faith. Then let them share how they think the prophet must have felt when the rain started.

Explain that it often happens that after one experiences a great spiritual high, a deep spiritual depression follows and that this is what happened to Elijah. Read 1 Kings 19:9-18 and give a brief lecture on the significance of how God did speak to the prophet and how he helped Elijah deal with that depression.

4. Refer to the "And So . . ." statements on the newsprint and state that these are the major emphases for this session.

5. Give each member a pencil and a sheet of paper and ask that each one chart some times of spiritual highs he/she has experienced—maybe after a revival, Youth retreat/camp, or after witnessing to a lost friend. Then suggest that they also identify times of depression. Permit those who will to share and also to explain what they did to overcome the depression. Read again the last "And So" statement. Stress that when one does the will of God, he never stands alone and that one plus God equals enough.

Close with a prayer, thanking God that he who makes possible spiritual highs and lows also equips us to deal with both.

Esther:

Making Choices

Esther 1:1-22; 2:1-23; 3:8-15; 4:7-17; 5:1-8; 8:7-8,15-17

B. J. Dean

The World of Royalty (Esther 1)

It had been quite a party—lasting 180 days! Following that little affair, the king decided that he wanted to have another party for the people in the capital city. After another week of showing off his wealth, feasting, and drinking, King Ahasuerus wanted to display another of his prized possessions: the beautiful Queen Vashti. She refused to be paraded in front of his drunken guests! No one—not even a queen—disobeyed a command from the king.

Imagine for a moment the position Vashti faced. In the harems of the Near East, the accepted role for the female was one of total subservience. Yet Vashti was not only refusing to obey her husband but also a husband who was king! Her reason for refusing is not given, but the fact is that she would not go. She had to have known that at the most such a decision could cost her her life and that the least it could cost would be her crown.

Look again at verses 13-22. Here was the king—the ruler of over 127 provinces—and he was so upset and frustrated over the actions of one woman that he did not know how to handle her or the situation. So he called in his wise men. That they certainly were! In order to help their king save face, they took what should have been a disagreement between husband and his wife and turned it into a national affair. These wise men had visions of wives all over the country (including their own!) suddenly having the courage to disobey their husbands. That would be a real catastrophe—a national disaster!

Naturally the king was a lot happier to know that he was not just upset because his wife had disobeyed him but because a national crisis was involved. There was only one logical, obvious solution: get a new, more obedient queen and also send out a royal decree that all wives—whatever their social status—would honor (meaning obey) their husbands! That should certainly have made all the men feel more secure!

The Search Is On (Esther 2:1-4,12-14)

It was not practical for the queen's throne to remain empty for too long, so a plan was presented to and accepted by the king. It would be similar to—

but more than—a beauty contest. The beautiful, young virgins from all over the country were to be brought to the palace. They would undergo a year of training in the proper behavior for a member of the royal court and of beautification procedures. After that year, each night a different young woman would be taken in to the king. The next morning she would be moved to the house of concubines with the possibility of never again seeing the king, or she could be the one chosen as queen.

This may be a difficult situation for contemporary youth to understand. A young woman was risking all of her life for the chance of becoming queen, and that future would be determined by how the king responded to her on the basis of only one night. She would not be free to resume her life back at home. From then on she would be kept as a concubine in the king's harem. That was quite a risk!

A Jewess Becomes Queen of Persia (Esther 2:5-11,15-23)

Esther's parents were dead, and she had been adopted and reared by her cousin Mordecai. They were Jews living in Persia because of the deportation of the Jews under Nebuchadnezzar.

Apparently Mordecai was a man of some importance and may have had a position near the gate of the palace.

Esther was so beautiful that she was among those selected to be taken to the king's palace for the contest for the queen. There her qualities were recognized by Hegai, the keeper of the women. He gave her special attention in her training, in her servants, and in her position in the house. Esther learned very well. She could follow instructions because this was the way she had been brought up (v. 20). Mordecai had told her not to reveal her Jewish background to anyone; she did not. Each day Mordecai checked on her welfare.

Finally the time came for Esther to spend her night with Ahasuerus. The maidens were allowed to take with them anything they thought would improve their chances with the king. Esther was a young woman who had very positive feelings about herself and her capabilities. She took with her only those things Hegai told her to take.

The king was captivated by Esther and made her his queen. Then followed a great feast in her honor. Later Esther learned from Mordecai that there was a plot against the king. She told Ahasuerus, crediting Mordecai for the information. The guilty men were executed, and the event was recorded in the king's chronicles.

The Evil Plot (Esther 3:8-15)

The Jews were different: they had different dietary laws, different ways of worshiping, a different God, maybe they even looked different. Some people have a difficult time accepting those who are different, and their solution is to get rid of those who don't fit their mold. Haman was like that. He really didn't like Jews, but what had really triggered his anger was Mordecai's refusal to bow down to Haman as he passed through the palace gates (v. 5).

Haman was second only to the king. When he presented to Ahasuerus his plan for getting rid of the Jewish people, the king didn't question him, didn't investigate the situation. He simply said, "If it seems like a good idea to you, it's okay with me." The order went out to the entire kingdom that on the thirteenth day of the twelfth month all Jews, both young and old, little children and women were to be killed. Why? They were Jews. Hitler's holocaust was not an original idea.

Save Your People, Esther (Esther 4:7-14)

Mordecai the Jew realized that immediate action was required if his people—God's chosen people—in Persia were going to be saved. He saw only one possibility: Esther.

He sent word to the queen to go to the king and request that he rescind that decree and save the Jewish people. Esther was hesitant to do that because there was a law that anyone who went into the king's inner court without invitation could be received in one of two ways: he could be put to death or the king could receive him. There was an additional reason for Esther's hesitancy: the king had not called for her presence for a month! She sent this message back to Mordecai.

Mordecai was a practical man. He sent another message to Esther that said in effect, "Think, Esther. The decree says all Jews. It does not exclude anyone who is in the king's household. You are a Jewess and that means you have already been condemned to death. If the king receives you, you have a chance. If he doesn't, you are no worse off."

One of the most powerful verses in the Old Testament is Esther 4:14. It is one every Christian should ask himself when he is facing difficult situations: "Who knows whether you have not come to the kingdom for such a time as this?" (4:14, RSV).

A Plan of Action (Esther 4:15-17; 5:1-8)

Although the name of God is not mentioned in the book of Esther, the request that Esther made of Mordecai and all the Jews indicates that she was very much aware of the power of God that can be released through prayer.

Esther heard Mordecai's plea, she had support from the prayers of the Jewish people, and the time had come for her to take action. She decided to stand for what was right, even if it cost her her life.

The queen carefully made her plans, and the king accepted her when she came into his court. At an especially prepared banquet where the only two guests were the king and Haman, Esther was able to convince Ahasuerus that Haman had misled him.

Mission Accomplished (Esther 8:7-8,15-17)

Esther pleaded her case well. The king rescinded his action, and God's people were more than saved—they were joyous and happy! Why? Because a young woman believed that she had come to the kingdom for that particular hour, and that belief gave her the courage to act.

And So . . .

There are many lessons to be learned from Esther, but in this study we have concentrated on three:

(1) With faith in God, courage, and determination, you can overcome and/or enrich the circumstances of your birth and early years.

(2) You should be willing to learn and then be obedient and loyal to that instruction which strengthens you in a life of service to God and others.

(3) When you recognize a wrong, you should be willing to take a stand—even at the risk of personal danger—to right that wrong.

SUGGESTIONS FOR LEADING THE BIBLE STUDY

Through a study of the life of Esther, youth can learn to make important decisions in situations they encounter in their lives.

Get Ready

Prepare a focal wall with large, colorful letters that spell out: ESTHER—MAKING IMPORTANT DECISIONS. On the wall, place the outline for the study and a large strip of butcher paper prepared according to the instructions in step 2. Put the "And So . . ." statements on a sheet of paper for step 4. Provide a pencil and a sheet of paper for each person.

Lead Bible Study

1. Share the following illustration. In February of 1981, it was announced that Prince Charles, heir to the throne of England, would marry Lady Diana Spencer in July. In a comic strip, a female police officer was sent to try and stop a suicide by a young woman here in the States who was about to jump from a high bridge. The officer asked her why she wanted to jump. Her reply was, "Prince Charles is marrying someone else! Now I'll never get to be Queen of England."

Ask the youth about how realistic this dream was. Tell the group to imagine that they are living in a foreign land where their families were taken as captives and then question them about how realistic it would be for one of the girls to imagine that she would one day be queen of that country. Then explain that this study is about just such a girl—and that if she ever dreamed about becoming queen, her dream came true.

2. Write the outline captions and references from the background material on the chalkboard or a piece of newsprint. Put a long strip of butcher paper on your focal wall, divide it into four columns, and label them *Ahasuerus, Mordecai, Esther,* and *Haman.*

Divide your group into four teams and assign each column to a team. Instruct the youth to listen to the lecture/discussion giving special attention to information about the character assigned to their group.

3. Using the outline, lead the group in a lecture/discussion of the biblical content. Secure involvement by allowing the youth to assist you in the telling of the story of Esther. After each section, allow each team to put up on the chart any new information gathered about their character. Your chart could look like the one below.

After the chart is completed, ask how many of the characteristics listed could apply to today's teenagers. Put a check by each one renamed.

4. Refer to "And So" in the background material for the truths to be learned from this session. Write these on a sheet of newsprint, allowing the youth to review how each of these applied to Esther. Then ask how these truths could apply to the lives of teenagers today.

5. Give each youth a sheet of paper and a pencil and tell them to write a letter to any one of the characters on the chart in today's study, explaining what the youth learned from this person and how that will help him/her live more positively today.

Allow some of the youth to share their letters. Close with a prayer of gratitude to God for including in his Word the stories of people whose lives can help us overcome our weaknesses.

AHASUERUS	MORDECAI	ESTHER	HAMAN
king, selfish, loved parties, weak, easily led, listened to those who said what he wanted to hear, willing to listen	Jewish, alert, loyally to family, loyal to the king, possessed leadership qualities, saw opportunities, had religious faith	adopted, beautiful, teachable, loyal, obedient, bright, courageous	bigot, leader, recognized his opportunities, ambitious, jealous

Jesus:
Resurrection Life (Easter)
John 20:1 to 21:25

Vince Smith

The season of spring is always accompanied by a sense of freshness and renewal. It is the new beginning that is so apparent in spring that adds a sense of expectancy to life's everyday routine. New life is all around during the spring season. Trees are budding. Grass is sprouting. Flowers are creeping from the earth with a sense of timidness as they take on a new glory and freshness. Spring is simply a season that allows persons to shed the cold of winter, the bundles of life and approach a new day and new season, with a new sensitivity to life in all of its meaning.

Jesus' Death Crushed Hope

For Jesus' disciples, the death of their teacher had dashed all of their hopes and dreams. The possibility that the Messiah had come seemed totally out of the question as they looked at the stone that so coldly and seemingly permanently sealed the borrowed tomb in which his body had been placed. The Gospel accounts reflect dashed hopes, broken spirits, distraught emotions, and feelings of ambivalence. Where once there had been light, now there was darkness. Where once there had been bread, now there was famine. Where once there had been a refreshing oasis, now there was a dry, parched, barren land. The end had come so quickly. Indeed, it was over. And, it all seemed to be so final, so completely futile, so shrouded in meaninglessness. For hours the disciples cowered behind emotional barriers that were more confining than the massive stones that formulated a Roman prison stockade. But God was not finished; indeed, he had only just begun. For, as he promised, Jesus walked out of the tomb, conquering death, fulfilling all the promises. Only hours before God's promises had seemed as worthless remembrances in the cluttered attic mind of a nostalgic disciple. Now, just as spring brings new life to God's creation, Jesus' resurrection can bring new life to God's choicest creation.

The whole idea of Easter is theological. Its meaning is found in the person of Jesus Christ, who when he was raised from the grave brought with him hope for all personkind. The Easter event is a basis of worship and the very reason that Christians gather together on the first day of the week. In reality, Easter is something believers celebrate fifty-two times a year!

Resurrection Affects Daily Living

But, the resurrection has several specifically practical implications for daily living. This study will examine four of those implications and seek to provide direction that will enable a believer to walk more faithfully and confidently because of the most crucial event in human history—the resurrection of Jesus Christ, the Easter event!

Abundant Life.—First, in John 10:10 (NIV) Jesus said, "I have come that they may have life, and have it to the full." The basic reason for Jesus' coming was that people needed a means by which victory, fullness, and abundance in life might be experienced. The Easter event resounds with victory. In this event, Jesus' victory became the victory of all persons who would put personal faith in him. The victorious Christian life is experienced as one denies self and allows the resurrection of Jesus Christ to find fullness in one's daily existence.

Victory does not mean there will not be times when Christians feel depressed, alone, and snared by life's circumstances. The victory means that amid the turbulence of daily life there is assurance that the ultimate victory has been won by Jesus Christ. In Jesus Christ is found both the present victory and the eternal victory.

Beginning Again.—Second, the Easter event reflects the ability to begin anew. In Jesus there is the opportunity to start all over. Jesus called this the new birth. It has been said that the Christian lives in "the land of beginning again." The ability to find forgiveness and to discover that one's mistakes are not eternal, unpardonable blotches on life is a basis for real joy. In Romans 14:8 (NIV), Paul wrote, "whether we live or die, we belong to the Lord." In Romans 8:38-39 (NIV), the apostle wrote, "For I am convinced that neither death nor life, neither angels nor demons, neither the present nor the future, nor any powers, neither height nor depth, nor anything else in all creation, will be able to separate us from the love of God that is in Christ Jesus our Lord."

Christians must never forget that they have not yet been made complete. Although born again, the perfection aspect of salvation is yet to come. Although it is necessary to live life today with an awareness of one's humanness and bent to sinning, the new beginning is always available to anyone that is willing to seek forgiveness, turn, and walk in a new direction. In reality, the Easter event allows a Christian to live in a perpetual season of spring since the resurrection power of Jesus abides in every Christian.

42

Overcoming Power

Third, the Easter event has provided a previously unavailable dynamic for life. When Jesus conquered death, he unleashed a power that enables his disciples to overcome the world. In the resurrection, Jesus overcame physical death, allowing us the opportunity to be the conqueror of spiritual death.

The power of the resurrection is best seen in the life of the apostle Peter. Peter denied Jesus on three occasions. But, following the resurrection and the coming of God the Holy Spirit, a new power enabled the once weak apostle to be a tower of strength and proclaim with intense assurance the lordship of Jesus Christ.

The power factor enables Christians today to overcome seemingly insurmountable roadblocks and hurdles. The believer's relationship with Jesus connects him with the resurrection power of Jesus (Eph. 1:19b-20). The power is in the person of Jesus Christ who lives in each Christian through the Holy Spirit. Every Christian should be certain of God's unchanging faithfulness and the resultant power that can be theirs if a faith response is made to the Christ of the Easter event.

Future Hope

Fourth, the Easter event reveals a future hope that is available today to all who believe. Following the resurrection, Jesus appeared to his disciples several times over a period of forty days. Each Gospel account provides insight into the postresurrection events. But, John 20—21 provide a glimpse of the emotion that captivated the disciples in those days. Each time Jesus appeared and spoke after his resurrection, he reiterated the hope that the disciples possessed because of their relationship with him. It is not surprising that Jesus' final days on earth would resound with victory and hope, for his entire ministry had carried that same theme.

The empty tomb, for the believer, is the sign that hopelessness has been shattered and genuine hope has been reinstated following the cross event. As important as the cross is theologically, it is the meaning of the empty tomb that shows the victory of the cross. If Jesus had not been raised from the dead, there would be no hope or meaning to anything Jesus had said or done in his earthly ministry. It would have been finished in hopelessness. But, rather than hopelessness, the Light of the world became the Living Hope for shattering the darkness of sin.

It must be remembered that the Easter event points dramatically to God's faithfulness. Hebrews 4:15 tells us that Jesus Christ, our high priest, is without sin. Persons can trust in Jesus Christ because of who he is. He is the only one who has ever completely conquered sin. And the Easter event points to his triumph over both sin and the grave. The victory was won on that Sunday morning when Jesus Christ walked out of the borrowed tomb as the living, risen, conquering Savior.

For the Christian, victory is found in the person of Jesus Christ. It is his enabling power that gives the new birth and provides the ability by which persons can face the difficulties of life with assurance and a positiveness that comes only from knowing the risen Lord. Were it not for the Easter event, Christianity would be a lifeless, empty, religious philosophy. Because of the Easter event, Christianity is a dynamic relationship with the resurrected Lord Jesus Christ.

Each year countless thousands of pilgrims make their way to Jerusalem and look into the empty tomb that tradition says is the spot where Jesus was laid after his death. But Christian pilgrims find no body, no grave clothes, no inscription with their founders name. All they find is an empty tomb. And that's the greatest find of all! They joyfully exclaim with the disciples of the first century—"He is alive, he is alive!" It is in his resurrection life that the victory is won today. Everyday is a celebration of Easter for the Christian.

SUGGESTIONS FOR LEADING THE BIBLE STUDY

From a study of the resurrection of Jesus, youth can learn that resurrection power can be theirs through faith in Jesus Christ.

Get Ready

Prepare the overview for step 1. You may want to write the question the youth are to answer on the chalkboard. You will need an index card and pencil for each youth. Enlist a reader for step 3, or be prepared to read yourself. If you choose to follow the alternate suggestion for step 3, preparation will need to be made beforehand. You may wish to provide pencil and paper for each group in step 4.

Lead Bible Study

1. Share with the youth an overview of John 20:1 to 21:25. Highlight the places that show Jesus' aliveness, providing power and hope for all that Christians are and do. Ask each youth to listen in order to be able to finish this statement: The most important thing about Jesus' resurrection to me is. . . . Give each youth a 3-x-5 index card and a pencil. Ask them to complete the sentence. If some of the youth will share what they have written, encourage them.

2. Ask the youth to read the following Scripture verses in their Bibles: John 10:10, Romans 8:38-39; 14:8; Ephesians 1:19b-20; Hebrews 4:15. Ask them to choose the verse they like best. Divide them into groups according to

verses and ask them to memorize the verse. After an appropriate time, ask each group to say their verse. Encourage the youth to incorporate the meaning of the passage into their daily lives during the next week and to share it with several others.

3. Ask: How do you think the disciples felt when they realized Jesus' body was no longer in the tomb? After most of the ideas are verbalized, have someone read John 20:1-18. Ask the youth to listen for any ideas not covered in the discussion. Now read John 20:19-29. Ask the youth to listen for the emotions shown when the disciples saw the risen Lord.

Alternate: This passage of John would be great for a role play by several youth. The Scripture itself could be used for parts. If you choose the role play, select youth ahead of time and work with them for effectiveness.

4. Conclude by asking, Why is Sunday a weekly celebration of Easter? (Since Jesus arose on the first day of the week, Sunday, the Christian day of worship was changed from Saturday, the sabbath. Christians worship a living Lord not a dead hero.) Divide the youth into several groups, according to the number you have. Ask each group to answer this question, How can we best celebrate the victory of Jesus' resurrection each Sunday? Call for reports. Conclude with a prayer of thanksgiving for a risen, living Lord who is the constant companion of every Christian.

Joseph:
Disappointment Need Not Be Defeat
Genesis 37:2-36; 39:1-23; 41:37-45; 45:1-8
Forrest W. Jackson

Jacob's Favoritism (37:2-11)

Jacob loved Rachel almost as much as he loved God. Rachel had always been his favorite. But Rachel had died giving birth to Joseph's brother, Benjamin. Jacob must have transferred his love for Rachel to Joseph, her older son. Jacob's love for Rachel and Joseph blinded him to his own favoritism. Jacob's favoritism was obvious to everyone, except himself. Jacob had learned little from his experience with the favoritism of his father for Esau and of his mother for himself.

Joseph was favored! There was no doubt about it. He was given a special "coat of many colours" (KJV) or "a long robe with sleeves" (RSV). Whatever else this garment signified, it meant that Joseph had special privileges. Joseph's brothers knew that Joseph had the largest share of their father's love. They hated him for it.

Joseph did two things that may have been influenced by Jacob's favoritism. Joseph told on his brothers for not doing what Jacob wanted them to do. He also shared his dreams which showed himself in a superior role to the rest of his family. The put-down of his brothers in his report to Jacob and his telling of his dreams completely cut Joseph off from his brothers. They not only hated him but could not even speak to him without a fuss (v. 4).

Joseph's Loss of Freedom (37:12-28)

Jacob either was blissfully unaware of the trouble between Joseph and his brothers or he felt they dared not harm his favorite son. Jacob was not the last father to believe he had more control over his family than he actually had. The lesson of life is that youth make their own choices when they are growing up. Often their decisions are the opposite of what parents would like.

Jacob sent Joseph to check on his brothers. It was the last time Jacob would see Joseph for a number of years.

Joseph found how uncertain life can be. One moment he walked free, a favorite of his father. The next moment he was lifted by the rough hands of his brothers and thrown into a pit. The pit into which Joseph was tossed was probably a cistern. It was dry and saved Joseph from drowning. On the other hand, its dryness meant he had no water to drink. Joseph's coat had been taken off, possibly to be used in mocking sport by his brothers.

The callousness of the brothers is seen in their sitting down to eat (v. 25) while Joseph was in the pit. By their own admission (42:21), Joseph was pleading with his brothers to let him go. But they just kept on eating.

The debate over whether the caravan was made up of Ishmaelites (v. 25) or Midianites (v. 28) or both will continue. But the main truth was that Joseph's brothers sold him into slavery.

Then one bad deed led to another. In order to cover their crime against Joseph, the brothers entered a conspiracy of silence and gave Jacob Joseph's bloody coat. Jacob assumed Joseph had been killed by some wild animal.

Joseph's Slavery (39:1-18)

Joseph's radical change from favorite son to slave must have been traumatic. It is hard to imagine how he coped. Joseph must have been sustained by his dream and his trust in God to bring it to pass. Joseph practiced the philosophy, "Do the best you can with what you have each day."

Since Joseph served God first and then Potiphar, he did a better job than the other slaves. Also God blessed Potiphar because of Joseph. God must have blessed Potiphar specifically by causing what Joseph did to make money for Potiphar. This was so unusual that Potiphar not only took notice but also made Joseph his chief steward (head honcho). Joseph knew that his rise to leadership was because "the Lord was with him" (vv. 3,21,23).

Potiphar wasn't the only one who noticed Joseph. Potiphar's wife also noticed that "Joseph was handsome and good-looking" (v. 6, RSV). Joseph obviously inherited Rachel's good looks (29:17). Potiphar's wife set out to seduce Joseph. The story is as modern as today's newspaper. The only difference is Joseph refused. Joseph, unlike many modern people, refused to have a sexual relationship with Potiphar's wife. His reasons for refusal can be very instructive for us.

First, Joseph respected people. His respect for Potiphar and the trust Potiphar had placed in him caused him to refuse. Joseph also reminded her that she was Potiphar's *wife*. Joseph must have respected Potiphar's wife for Potiphar's sake if not her own.

Second, Joseph believed that sexual relations outside of marriage was a "great wickedness" (v. 9). It was not a joking matter. It was not a subject for magazines and other media to use and make outrageous profits. It was wickedness.

Third, Joseph also saw the wickedness as "sin against God" (v. 9, TEV).

Joseph's relationship to God helped him make right decisions. Too many people who call themselves Christians fail to have a right relationship with God. A right relationship with God means that a person cannot live a life of habitual sin. And a sexual relationship outside of marriage is sin.

Joseph could have asked, Why not? Who would know? She could cause me to lose my job, couldn't she? (This question could be especially interesting to a person with a dream like Joseph's.) What's wrong with using sex for advancement? Joseph was not the first to face these questions. Nor was he the last. Potiphar's wife used every trick in the book. She appealed to Joseph's passion, his pride, his loneliness and hurt, and his desire for advancement.

Joseph had already decided about right and wrong. He did not wait for the passionate moment to decide. He knew that sex outside marriage was sin. And he had decided he would not sin.

Joseph's Imprisonment (39:19-23)

Joseph must have thanked God for the strength to resist sexual temptation. He must have thought, *How pleased Potiphar will be.* But he was naive. He underestimated the anger of Potiphar's wife. She accused Joseph of attempted rape. Potiphar threw Joseph into prison. (I personally feel that Potiphar would have killed Joseph if he had believed his wife. However, the biblical writer doesn't comment on that question.)

This must have been a great blow to Joseph. He had done what was right. He had done the moral and godly thing. And he was thrown into prison! Where was God? In moments like that a person will become much better or very much worse.

Joseph's philosophy of life won again over whatever depression he must have had after being put into prison. He would continue to trust God. He would be the best prisoner he could be. He would wait for God to act. It took God "two whole years" (41:1) to act. Joseph finally received his audience before Pharaoh, who could make his dreams come true.

Joseph's Dream Came True (41:37-49)

God gave Joseph the interpretation of Pharaoh's dream. None of Pharaoh's magicians and wise men could make any sense of his dream. Joseph made it clear that "God had revealed" (v. 25) the dream to Pharaoh through Joseph.

Pharaoh was so impressed that he gave Joseph the number two position in Egypt. The "signet ring," "garments of fine linen," "a gold chain," and Pharaoh's "second chariot" (vv. 42-43) were all symbols of Joseph's new authority. Joseph's dream had come true. At Pharaoh's command, everyone would "bow the knee!" (v. 43, RSV).

Joseph's grain conservation program paid off. The famine brought people from many countries to Egypt for grain. Even Joseph's brothers came. Thus began Joseph's greatest temptation.

Joseph's Forgiveness (45:1-8)

Joseph tested his brothers to see if they had changed. The Bible is silent concerning what happened to Joseph's brothers during these years. Evidently their experiences had changed them to some degree. Perhaps their own consciences had brought about some change, for they were still dealing with their guilt when they came before Joseph (42:21-22).

Joseph's misfortunes had been used by himself and God to bring him to full maturity in a way that pleased God. Joseph was now ready for this test. He freely forgave his brothers. Joseph said, "I am your brother, Joseph, whom you sold into Egypt. And now do not be distressed, or angry with yourselves, because you sold me here; for God sent me before you to preserve life" (vv. 4-5, RSV).

Forgiveness is the mark of a person in a right relationship with God. It is the ultimate grace between people. A forgiving spirit marks a person as being like God.

Joseph had become the kind of person whom God could make his dream come true. Joseph was not a person who would use his greatness only for personal benefit. He would not be puffed up by seeing others bow before him. He realized that God had "made me a father to Pharaoh, and lord of all his house and ruler of all the land of Egypt" (v. 8, RSV).

Joseph did not let disappointment defeat him. He believed that God worked in everything that happened to him to bring good out of it for him (Rom. 8:28, RSV). "The Lord was with Joseph" (Gen. 39:21), and Joseph believed that God would work out his purpose in Joseph's life. The belief that God is working out his purpose in your life will enable you to keep disappointments from becoming defeats in your personal life.

SUGGESTIONS FOR LEADING BIBLE STUDY

From a study of the life of Joseph, youth can learn that disappointments need not be defeat.

Get Ready

Prepare the lecture for step 1. Have pencils and paper ready for step 2. Be sure to have felt-tip pens and sufficient butcher paper for step 3. Read through steps 4 and 5. Be familiar with the background material for leading the discussions.

Lead Bible Study

1. Ask, Have you ever owned anything that was a favorite of yours? Allow several youth to name their favorite. Then ask, What made it a favorite? Lead the youth to work up a definition of the word *favorite*. Write the definition on the chalkboard.

Using the material under "Jacob's Favoritism (37:2-11)" and "Joseph's Loss of Freedom (37:12-28)," recount the story of Joseph to the point of his being sold as a slave. Be sure to emphasize Joseph's dream that he would someday be great and powerful.

2. Ask the youth to read Genesis 39:1-18 in their Bibles. Give them a pencil and a sheet of paper. Ask them to read back through the passage and decide how Joseph's relationship to God affected how he related to Potiphar and his wife. Ask them to write their answer in a short paragraph. When they have finished, ask several youth to share their paragraphs. Be alert for opportunities to help the youth understand that their relationships with God should affect the way they live and relate to people.

3. Divide your youth into two groups. Give each group a felt-tip pen and a large sheet of butcher paper. Ask them to attach their butcher paper to the wall. Let each group choose someone to do the writing and to make the report. Ask group 1 to write on their sheet the reasons being sold as a slave was a disappointment to Joseph. Also ask them to list the reasons Joseph did not allow this disappointment to defeat him. Ask group 2 to record the reasons being put into prison was a disappointment for Joseph. Also ask them to list the reasons Joseph did not let this disappointment defeat him. When they have finished, call for reports from each group. When the reports are completed, ask, What can we learn from Joseph that will help us to know that our disappointments need not defeat us?

4. Instruct the youth to read Genesis 41:37-49; 45:1-8. Then ask, Why was Joseph's greatest temptation after he became second to Pharaoh? (Joseph had absolute power to get revenge on his brothers, Potiphar and his wife, and anyone he had a problem with.) Now ask, What does a forgiving spirit have to do with being a great person? (One who forgives is like God and cares for others.)

5. Close by encouraging youth not to let their disappointments defeat them. Encourage them to be faithful to God, forgiving toward others, and believing in themselves. Challenge them to dream great things and believe that God will work for good in everything that happens to them. Close with prayer. Ask God to be personally present with each youth in such a way that the disappointments that will surely come will not defeat them.

Joshua:

Decision Making

Numbers 13:8,16 to 14:10; 27:18-23; Joshua 6:1-21; 10:1-11;
11:1-9,16-23; 24:1,14-28

Dan G. Kent

A pastor once told me his church had made only one decision in fourteen years. They had decided not to decide.

How foolish! They may not have thought they were making decisions, and they may have been calling what they were doing by some other name, but they were deciding just the same.

We all make all kinds of decisions, all the time. Some matter little: which shoes to wear. Some matter much: which values to live by.

Yes, we all are constantly making decisions, sometimes by default, sometimes without realizing it, sometimes without meaning to. As one wise man said, even not to decide is to decide.

If decision making is so constant and pivotal, we need to study about a person who can help us make decisions in the best possible way.

Deciding About the Truth (Num. 13:8,16 to 14:10)

Joshua began to move to center stage as one of the twelve spies Moses sent to reconnoiter the Promised Land (Num. 13:8,16). These men were to see what the land was like, how numerous and strong the people were, and what kind of settlements they lived in (13:18-20). The spies did so. They looked Canaan over completely. After forty days, they returned with a report, including some of the rich fruit of the land for show and tell (13:23-27).

The spies claimed to have fulfilled their commission. They had found out that the land was a rich one. However, they also reported that the people were strong. Their cities were large and well fortified. Some of the people were giants (13:27-28). That was quite a scouting report, wasn't it? The implication was that the land could not be taken.

Caleb, Joshua's comrade, disagreed. He said they should, by all means, go up and take the land. He said they were well able to do so (13:30). The majority of the spies argued. In fact, they even changed their story to exaggerate the difficulties they had encountered. They called Canaan a land that devoured its inhabitants. They claimed that *all* the people of the land were giants (13:31-33).

Like Caleb, Joshua had made a decision about the truth. He decided to speak the truth, even if everyone disagreed with him. He wouldn't be swayed by majority vote. He decided to stand by the truth even if it was dangerous to do so. He and Caleb reaffirmed their positive, optimistic report. They further said that if the Lord were pleased with the people, he could give them the land despite any difficulties.

The congregation was ready to stone them to death. It was a good thing Joshua had already made his decision about the truth.

Deciding About Leadership (Num. 27:18-23)

With Moses getting on up in years, the time finally came for someone to be set aside to take his place. Of course, Joshua became that one. Moses was a hard act to follow, but Joshua was the logical one to do it.

The Lord called Joshua a man indwelt by his Spirit. He told Moses to take him and lay his hand on him. He was to have him stand before Eleazar, the son of Aaron who had become the high priest, and also before all the congregation. In that public setting, Moses was to commission Joshua (27:18-19).

From then on Joshua was to share Moses' authority. The congregation was to look to him as their leader. He was to depend on Eleazar's help in determining the Lord's will in specific situations. He was to command the people as they went out and came in (27:20-21).

We might call this Joshua's inauguration, or even his ordination. He led the people militarily in their long conquest of Canaan (Deut. 1:38; 3:28). He was a leader of worship, as we see in Joshua 8:30-35. He led both by word and by example.

Joshua is one of the unsung heroes of the Bible. He was far more important than we usually realize. He may have been as important in his day as Moses was in his. This is partly because he had made the right decision about leadership.

We all lead, in one way or another. We all lead, and we all follow. We all have influence. We all affect others.

So did Joshua. Remember, Moses did not lead the Israelites into the Promised Land; Joshua did.

Deciding About Trust (Josh. 6:1-21)

There were many, many times during Joshua's life when he had to make decisions about trust and dependence on the Lord. One of the most pivotal of these came when his army faced the formidable fortress of Jericho.

Joshua was a courageous man, and the Lord assured him in advance that he would win the victory (6:2), but we ought to know from experience that we have to make a deliberate decision to act on the Lord's promises.

Have you ever stopped to consider the implications of the instructions the Lord gave? Joshua was not to attack Jericho; instead, he and his people were to march around the city. (Can't you see him gulp at the thought of having to pass these instructions on to his men?)

And then what? They were to do it again the next day. And then what? They were to do it again. And so on it went until the seventh day, when they were to . . . you guessed it, march around the city seven times (6:3-4). A stranger military strategy the world has never known. It must have been a strain on Joshua's decision to trust the Lord.

But what the Lord said, Joshua tried his best to do. (I also wonder what the defenders of Jericho thought about all this. The approaching enemy did not attack them. Instead they gave them the "silent treatment." It was what we today would call psychological warfare.)

The people kept quiet, as Joshua commanded (6:10). Led by the priests carrying the ark of the covenant, they and the army moved around the city as instructed. Then, after the seventh circuit on the seventh day, Joshua commanded them to "Shout! For the Lord has given you the city" (6:16, NASB).

The people shouted, the priests blew their rams' horn trumpets, and the Lord leveled the walls of that fortress. The Lord got the credit for the victory because he had done all the work. However, it is also important that Joshua had decided to trust the Lord.

Deciding About Hard Work (Josh. 10:1-11; 11:1-9,16-23)

Have you ever heard the old advice about trusting as if everything depended on the Lord and working as if everything depended on you? Joshua did exactly that. He trusted implicitly as we saw in chapter 6. He also worked as hard as he could.

Chapters 10 and 11 describe Joshua's southern and northern campaigns of conquest, after he had secured the central section of the country (chs. 6—9). The two stories of the two campaigns are quite similar, and both of them are stories of hard work.

Chapter 9 tells how Gibeon and the other cities in the Gibeonite league allied themselves with the invading Israelites. This incensed the other Canaanite cities in the southern part of Palestine. The kings of those cities could at last clearly read the handwriting on the wall. They realized that they were going to have to band together to resist Joshua or it would be too late. (To tell the truth, it was already too late.)

The kings of Jerusalem, Hebron, and several other places attacked Israel's new ally, Gibeon. The Gibeonites appealed to Joshua for help. That gave him just the opportunity he had been wanting. He gathered his troops and began a forced march to break the siege (10:1-7).

Once again the Lord promised Joshua the victory (10:8). However, despite such a promise, Joshua had made an important decision about hard work. He and his men marched all night, across twenty miles of rugged terrain. This is how he was able to come upon the enemy suddenly. The Lord confounded them before Israel, as Joshua and his determined force caught them completely by surprise. The victory was sudden, and it was also complete (10:9-11).

Chapter 11 tells a parallel story; only the geographical setting is different. Jabin, the king of Hazor, gathered other kings of the north in a huge coalition of forces (11:1-5). Again the Lord gave a promise of victory (11:6). Again Joshua and his men worked hard. They attacked suddenly and fiercely (11:7). And again the Lord gave the victory (11:8-9). This is how Joshua took the entire land. He waged war a long time. He fought hard until the victory came (11:16-23).

I once heard that the harder you work the luckier you get. That was one of Joshua's secrets. He had made an important decision about hard work. No wonder he was so "lucky."

Deciding About Example (Josh. 24:1,14-28)

Our study concludes with another account of Joshua as leader. At the end of his life, he led the people in a great, covenant renewal ceremony at the sanctuary at Shechem. One way he showed leadership was in setting the example of fully following the Lord (Num. 32:12).

The new generation that had completed the conquest of the land gathered before the Lord (Josh. 24:1). Joshua reminded them of the mighty acts of the Lord and how gracious the Lord had been to them (24:2-13). He appealed to them to put away all the false gods that had been worshiped by their ancestors and their neighbors. He urged them to choose that very day whom they would serve (24:14-15).

"As for me and my house," Joshua said, "we will serve the Lord" (24:15, NASB). Once again, Joshua had made a decision. Here he was also leading others to make the right decision. He was urging others to make the right decision. He was setting the right kind of example, the kind that would influence family members and others.

When the people responded to Joshua's example, he did everything he could to reinforce their decision (24:16-24). He led them in a formal ceremony of covenant renewal. He recorded the entire proceedings. He made the occasion as solemn and impressive as he could (24:25-28).

Joshua could hardly have led the people, could he, if he had not first taken that step himself? The beginning of their experiences with the Lord was the example set by his own decision of commitment.

SUGGESTIONS FOR LEADING THE BIBLE STUDY

From a study of the life of Joshua, youth can learn to make important decisions that will affect their spiritual life and growth.

Get Ready

For step 1 you will need felt-tip pens and a sheet of newsprint. Prepare the written assignments for teams 1, 3, and 5 in step 2. You will also need to enlist two people for reports 2 and 4 in step 2. For step 3 you will need a chalkboard and chalk, or some other writing surface, along with pencils and paper for each youth.

Lead Bible Study

1. Create interest in the study by asking, How many of you have decided about something since you entered the study area? Ask the youth to name the different decisions they have made since entering, while two youth use felt-tip pens to list the decisions on a sheet of newsprint. Be ready to suggest any decisions overlooked, such as where to sit, whom to sit by, and whether to move the chair.

Point out that since we all make decisions, and since we do so constantly, we need to spend some time studying about a person who can help us with our decision making.

2. Lead the youth to examine the Bible for themselves by organizing them into three activity groups (or multiples of three if the groups are too large). Distribute the following written assignments. Note the two individual assignments. After ten minutes, call for reports.

Team 1, Deciding about the truth. Create a brief skit portraying the events of Numbers 13:16 to 14:10 and Joshua's role in them. Be ready to share your skit with the entire class. Be ready to lead the other youth in thinking about decisions Joshua had to make in this instance.

Team 3, Deciding about trust. Pretend you were citizens of Jericho, preparing to defend your city against attack by Joshua and his troops. Describe the events of Joshua 6:1-21 from your standpoint. Include your feelings at each point. Also include your impressions of the Israelite leader and the decisions he had to make. Be ready to report to the entire class.

Team 5, Deciding about example. Pretend you were one of the people gathered before Joshua and the Lord at Shechem, as described in Joshua 24:1,14-18. Describe the events of this passage from your standpoint. Include your feelings at each point. Also include your impressions of your leader, Joshua, and the decisions he himself had to make. Be ready to report to the entire class.

For report 2, enlist in advance someone who has surrendered to Christian service to briefly describe the events of Numbers 27:18-23 from the standpoint of the sense of the Lord's call in one's own life.

For report 4, enlist in advance a mature adult to briefly describe the events of Joshua 10:1-11; 11:1-9,16-23 from the standpoint of his sense of the importance of hard work.

3. Help youth toward the application of Bible truth by asking them to name important decisions they are facing, or will be facing in the next three to five years, while you list them on a chalkboard. Be ready to add other suggestions, such as how they will spend the money they make on their jobs, what kind of students they will be, and how they will conduct themselves on dates.

Explain that the rest of the activity will be private. Ask each youth to select one of the decisions named and:

1. Write out on a sheet of paper the many different ways the decision chosen may be faced. (For instance, with college: what type of school, where, major, conduct on campus, studies, financing).

2. Write a second paragraph about how the different aspects of the decision will affect the youth's relationship with the Lord and relationships with others.

Conclude with a time of silent prayer. Urge each youth to ask the Lord for guidance in facing the particular decision, strength and courage in the making of it, and faithfulness in following through on it.

Mary and Martha:

Questioning to Find Answers
Luke 10:38-42; John 11:1-8,17-28,32-36,41-44

Kathryn Griffin

There had been a death. Members of the family were plunged into grief. "Why?" they kept asking. "Why did God let this happen?" "What have we done to deserve this?" "He was a good man. He never did anybody any harm."

What were they to do next? He had been their breadwinner, their support. They were not qualified to make a living for themselves. Their lives had centered around him. It was all they had wanted. Besides, what was there to do in their small town?

Night was approaching. It was a reminder of the good times they had shared. In the cool of the evening, they would sit under the trees and talk of life in the village. Or they would tell what they had done throughout the day and maybe swap tales of the neighbors. All of that was a thing of the past now. Death had a way of finalizing things, of erasing them from existence.

Jesus had known of Lazarus' illness. But he hadn't come. He had stayed where he was for two whole days. By the time he got to Bethany, Lazarus had been in his grave for four days.

Jesus wept. Even though he knew Lazarus would live again, he identified with his friends' grief. Did he know what it was like to be cut off from somebody he loved? Did he understand the agony of loneliness and hopelessness? Did he grieve because people failed to understand the nature of the resurrection and life after death, or did he grieve because he understood what it was to love and lose and to experience the full gamut of human emotions?

Everyone grieves. Sometimes it's because of a death. Sometimes it's because of losses of another kind. We all wonder why things happen to us. Questioning is a way of life. It's the way we go about finding answers for ourselves.

Before Lazarus Died

Now it came to pass, as they went, that he entered into a certain village: and a certain woman named Martha received him into her house. And she had a sister called Mary, which also sat at Jesus' feet, and heard his word.

But Martha was cumbered about much serving, and came to him, and said, Lord, dost thou not care that my sister hath left me to serve alone? bid her therefore that she help me. And Jesus answered and said unto her, Martha, Martha, thou art careful and troubled about many things: But one thing is needful: and Mary hath chosen that good part, which shall not be taken away from her (Luke 10:38-42).

Mary, Martha, and Lazarus were special friends of Jesus. Apparently he went to their home often. He was comfortable in their midst. He felt welcome. They valued his presence.

The incident recorded by Luke occurred after Jesus had "steadfastly set his face to go to Jerusalem." His mission was nearing its end. Suffering and death were ahead. The things he had tried to teach had been only partially understood. He had accomplished only a fraction of what he had hoped to accomplish. He would be forced to leave the future of the Christian movement in the hands of human beings whose training had been brief and who were hampered by the limitations of their humanity. As God's representative—as the living, visible demonstration of the invisible God—he must have wanted to show the world so much more about his Father's nature. His heart must have been heavy. He needed a friend.

How much Jesus shared with Mary and Martha and Lazarus, we have no way of knowing. Mary was willing to sit at his feet and learn from him. She knew that he was God. She understood his powers. At the time of her brother's death, she said to Jesus, in effect, "If you had been here, it wouldn't have happened." At least she understood to some degree that he had power over death. Maybe she had the privilege of many special revelations. Maybe she was a friend, a rare kind of kindred soul, with whom Jesus could share many of his innermost thoughts and concerns.

Martha, on the other hand, may not have been a talker. She may have been the "take charge" kind. While the other members of the family were enjoying their guests, she may have been happy to be preparing the meals and looking after everybody's welfare.

On the day in question, however, she was annoyed with Mary. She wanted Jesus to make Mary help her. But Jesus gently pointed out that Mary had chosen the better part, for that particular time, at any rate.

There are times when cooking meals and looking after our friends' physical needs are important. There are other times, however, when listening and sharing concerns is the most important thing to do. Jesus reminds us that we need to be sensitive to the particular needs that people have. We need to understand when the sharing of ourselves is more important than the sharing of our possessions.

Our friend Lazarus sleepeth; but I go, that I may awake him out of sleep. . . . Then when Jesus came, he found that he had lain in the grave four days already. . . . Then said Martha unto Jesus, Lord, if thou hadst been here, my brother had not died. But I know, that even now, whatsoever thou wilt ask of God, God will give it thee. . . . Then when Mary was come where Jesus was, and saw him, she fell down at his feet, saying unto him, Lord, if thou hadst been here, my brother had not died (John 11:11b,17, 21-22,32).

If Things Had Been Different

The word *if,* the grammarians teach us, indicates a condition contrary to the fact. It's almost a wish. It may border on an accusation. It may present a possibility. But always, it implies that the facts in the case are different from what they might have been.

"If you had been here," Mary and Martha told Jesus, "our brother wouldn't have died." But Jesus wasn't there.

"If my wife hadn't gotten sick," the man said as he applied for bankruptcy status, "I could have made it." But she did get sick, and the bills were astronomical.

"If I hadn't lost my balance," the little boy said as he surveyed the shattered glass, "the ball wouldn't have gone anywhere near that window." It was the ground's fault. There was a little mound at the boy's feet that shouldn't have been there. But he had to pay.

If I had made this or that choice, tne professional person says from the depths of depression, I wouldn't be in this dilemma. If we hadn't let him cross the street or drive to the beach or attend the party or play soccer or any one of a countless number of other things, bereaved parents often tell themselves, our child would still be alive.

We use the word all the time. *If . . . If . . If . . .* We use it in panic. We use it in disgust. We say it in disbelief. It speaks of remorse. It hints of an unnamed longing. It's a frustration word. It's a heartache word. It's an angry word. It comes up from the roots of our being.

"Why, Lord?" we ask. "Why did it have to be this way?" "Why did he have to die?" "Paralysis!? But why? It isn't fair! Say it isn't so!" "Divorce? I don't believe I'm hearing this! What have I done?" Why? Why couldn't it be different? What have we done to deserve it? We don't want to live any more. Life has gone sour. We had such hopes. If only . . . If only . . . If only . . . Things could have been so different.

When Jesus therefore saw her weeping, and the Jews also weeping which came with her, he groaned in the spirit, and was troubled, And said,

Where have ye laid him? They said unto him, Lord, come and see. Jesus wept. Then said the Jews, Behold how he loved him! (John 11:33-36).

Jesus Wept

Jesus cared for Lazarus. He was God and he had human feelings. His feet got dirty in the hot dust as he walked the road to Bethany. They had to be washed, just like everybody else's feet. He knew hunger and fatigue. Jesus loved. He experienced rejection. Whenever he spoke of loneliness, it was from the perspective of one who knew what he was talking about. He knew all about grief and suffering. He knew how to put himself in other people's places. He was a "people" himself.

God cares. When we hurt, he hurts. He made us with the capacity to grow, to fail, to succeed, to fall on our faces, to pick ourselves up and to rise above our limitations. We're made in his image. He knows what it's all about. He put a part of himself into our natures. Because we're part God—because he lives in us—we can be victorious. That's what Jesus' death was all about.

> "I am the resurrection, and the life: he that believeth in me, though he were dead, yet shall he live: And whosoever liveth and believeth in me shall never die. Believest thou this? She saith unto him, Yea, Lord: I believe that thou art the Christ, the Son of God, which should come into the world" (John 11:25-27).

What Death Teaches Us

Jesus had power over death, both his own and other people's. Jesus' own death was to be excruciatingly painful. But he was willing to experience it because of the inexpressibly joyful message he had to impart: There was to be a resurrection.

Lazarus experienced a literal resurrection. It taught a lesson, but it didn't have the power that Jesus' resurrection was to have. Resurrection makes all the difference. It gives meaning to life. It helps us understand immortality.

Life is full of deaths. We must die to childhood. We must die to our children's childhoods and dependency. We must bury them in their own special kinds of graves. We must die to self-centeredness. We must separate ourselves from stages of growth and from outworn concepts and bury them in their graves.

But the exciting part of it all is the resurrections. There are millions of them. The resurrected life is so much better than the old one.

That's the "why" of it all. We die in order to live again. Like Martha of Bethany, we don't understand it completely, but we believe it to be true.

SUGGESTIONS FOR LEADING THE BIBLE STUDY

From a study of the lives of Mary and Martha, youth can learn that questioning to find answers will strengthen their faith.

Get Ready

Prepare the assignments for step 1. Follow the directions in step 2 for preparing the chalkboard or a piece of newsprint. Be prepared to lead step 3. Step 4 will need some added preparation including your hymnal.

Lead Bible Study

1. Create an interest in and an understanding of the lesson to be learned from a study of Mary, Martha, and Lazarus by distributing the following assignments and calling for reactions and sharing of answers. (1) A question I've always wanted to ask God is, Why . . . (2) The thing most people don't understand about the Christian life is . . . (3) I most often use the word *if* when . . . (4) Adults are apt to question God concerning . . . (5) Youth most often question God concerning . . . (6) Children most often question God concerning . . . (7) The biggest uncertainty in my life is . . . (8) The reason I most need a close friend is . . . (9) The Christian truth I am most certain about is . . .

2. Using columns on the chalkboard labeled *Why, If,* and *I'm Sure,* lead youth to pull together comments that have been made on questions people ask God, the various kinds of *if* situations in our lives, and the Christian truths we're certain of.

3. Call for a reading of Luke 10:38-42 and John 11:1-8,17-28,32-36, 41-44. Ask youth to describe the relationship between Jesus and the Bethany family, to summarize the events surrounding Lazarus' death, to explain why the raising of Lazarus was dangerous to Jesus personally (see John 11:45 *ff.*), and to state the new concept Jesus hoped to get across concerning death. Lead youth also to state the benefits of close friendships, to verbalize the reasons why death (other people's) is traumatic and why many people may fear death for themselves, and to list kinds of symbolic deaths and resurrections people experience throughout their lifetimes. Lead youth to reflect also on the various kinds of grief they may have experienced or may expect to experience. (If resources such as Westberg's *Good Grief,* Claypool's *Stages in the Life of a Fellow Struggler,* and Booher's *The Faces of Death* are available, encourage the youth to read them.) A later discussion about the stages of grief and ways to handle and profit from it would make an excellent follow-up to this session.

4. Lead youth to share Scripture verses that offer assurance in troubled times. As they suggest titles, intersperse the singing of songs of reassurance with the Scripture verses and some sentence prayers regarding concerns, questions, and longings the youth may have.

Miriam:

Sibling Relationships

Exodus 1:1 to 2:10

Vince Smith

Keith and Mark were brothers. And, as brothers will often do, they spatted, squabbled, and rowdily fussed with each other. There was constant picking at each other, often mercilessly. It did not matter what the issue. If Mark stood on the left, Keith stood on the right! In everyday life, the brothers would disagree over what television station to turn to, who had a particular "toy" first, or who was going "offsides" by invading the private domain of the other's room.

Siblings Often Compete

From the beginning of time, brothers and sisters have disagreed, often disagreeably. The first murder, as recorded in Genesis 4 was the result of sibling rivalry. Even the sons of Noah, blessed as they were by God, brought the wrath of God upon their family as a result of improper relationships with each other and their father.

Twentieth-century psychologists tell us that competition between children in the same family is to be expected. The authorities point out that often parents inject rivalry into the relationships between their children by being insensitive to the needs that each child reflects. It is wrong to expect brothers and sisters to think alike or act alike. Each person is an individual. In the same way, it is unfair to make generalizations regarding siblings. An individual's personal worth must be affirmed and accentuated. Interdependence yes, but a drone no. If families are going to be healthy, happy, and Spirit-filled, brothers and sisters must work together to bring about the deepest desires of God for their particular family group. Brothers and sisters have a unique responsibility, because of their relationship, to discover under God's leading his will not only for their individual lives but also for the life of their family.

The Old Testament speaks of many family relationships and sibling rivalries. One thinks of Cain and Abel; Joseph and his brothers; Isaac and Ishmael; Noah's three sons—Shem, Ham, and Japheth; and the rivalry of Jacob and Esau. But no sibling relationship better illustrates the good and bad that can be accomplished like the triad of Moses, Aaron, and their sister, Miriam. Indeed, Miriam is the person on whom this study will key. It is only because of the long shadows cast by her brothers that her place in Old Testament history is not acclaimed more profoundly.

Miriam Was Responsible

Miriam was the daughter of Jochebed and the sister of Moses and Aaron. Later Jewish legends present her as the eldest of the three. Although not mentioned by name, she is presented in Exodus 2:3-8 as watching after the basket into which Jochebed placed her infant son, Moses. Miriam's responsibility was to watch the basket, to ensure its safety, and to know by whom it was discovered. Ultimately, Miriam secured her own mother to serve as the nurse for the baby discovered by Pharaoh's daughter in the bulrushes. That baby was Miriam's infant brother.

Miriam's early life is not the only portion mentioned in the Scriptures. She is also remembered as a "prophetess" in connection with her song of victory on the occasion of the crossing of the Red Sea by the Hebrews, as they departed Egypt and embarked upon their journey to the land God had promised (see Ex. 15:20-21). Yet her memory is not completely without tarnish. When her brother Moses married the Cushite woman, Miriam led a rebellion against her brother. Along with Aaron, Miriam claimed to be an oracle of God. But God rebuked them both. Miriam was struck with leprosy. It was only as the result of Moses' intercession that she was healed after a seven-day quarantine period (see Num. 12). Miriam is not mentioned again until the occasion of her death and burial at Kadesh, as recorded in Numbers 20:1. In later times the prophet Micah (see 6:4) remembered Miriam as a leader sent by God.

Principles for Testing Sibling Relationships

The events that formulate the biblical narrative of this Old Testament family present several principles by which relationships among brothers and sisters may be tested and evaluated. The lives of Miriam, Moses, and Aaron produced an intriguing case-study as to how siblings can support, strengthen, and reinforce meaningfully positive relationship traits. In this study, traits will be examined which have the potential of enhancing relationships among family members, specifically siblings.

Abiding Concern.—Miriam demonstrated an abiding concern for her infant brother, Moses. This personality trait, that made itself known early in Miriam's life, was to show itself often throughout her years. Truly, Miriam placed the welfare of Moses preeminent in her mind. Any number of excuses could have flooded into the mind of Miriam when instructed by her mother to stand at a distance and carefully watch for what would happen to the small papyrus basket holding the young child Moses. The favor of the Egyptians was certainly not upon the Israelites and spying on Pharaoh's daughter could, indeed, be dangerous business. Yet, without obvious fear and with a degree of admirable determination, Miriam watched the bobbing basket among the reeds. It was not enough for Miriam that her concern enabled her to quietly hide in waiting and watch. When her brother was discovered, Miriam, a Hebrew slave-girl, was immediately at the site asking the daughter of the Egyptian Pharaoh if she should not enlist the services of a Hebrew woman to serve as the young child's nurse. Brave, bold, unnerving, unimpeded all describe Miriam's actions. But the reason she could reflect such openness was because of an apparent, deep abiding concern for the welfare of her brother.

Brothers and sisters, in many families, simply "put up with each other." Miriam was genuinely concerned. In fact, she placed the welfare of Moses before her own safety. She had no guarantee that the daughter of Pharaoh would receive her kindly or affirm her surface brashness at making a suggestion to royalty! Putting another's welfare above our own well-being is a trait that family members would do well to emulate. Few persons today give any thought to another before looking out for the interests of self. Had Miriam lived by the old cliche, "If you don't look out for yourself, no one else will," Hebrew history might have been radically changed. Moses, at his most formative stage in life, might have been uninfluenced by his own godly mother.

Knowing Yourself.—Miriam demonstrated the advantage of knowing yourself. Miriam is not seen in the Exodus account as existing in the shadow of her famous brothers, Moses and Aaron. She realized her own worth as an individual and demonstrated her ability to develop her own gifts and personality. Today, many brothers or sisters believe they must play "second fiddle" to a more gifted, better athlete, or smarter brother or sister. The result is self-pity and feelings of personal inadequacy. Miriam is never presented in the Scriptures as one who felt she was worthless. Instead, Miriam was up front, leading the way, singing the praises of God and acknowledging the leadership roles of her brothers. Envy was absent, and in its place was an intense supportive affirmation. This sister, rather than saying, "See I'm not Moses, I'm just Miriam—and nobody even realizes I'm alive," sought to walk beside her brothers. In acknowledging another's worth, Miriam possessed the power to bless herself with joy, fulfillment, and contentment.

To be all that God would have ME to be should be the goal of every modern believer. True, you aren't Billy Graham, but if God had desired two Billy Grahams he could have created them. Instead, God created you—and only one of you—and if God loses you, there is no replacement. Miriam would say, "I am created in the image of God and all the Moseses in the world could not keep me from becoming all that God wants me to be."

Jealousy Sours Relationships.—The sibling interrelationships of Aaron, Moses, and Miriam point to the fact that jealousy can turn sweet water sour. A city known for its delicious water was shocked by the sudden insipid taste of its water. The hot summer had enabled algae to grow that the filters of the water treatment systems did not remove. The presence of the algae gave a horrible taste to what was normally refreshing water. Jealousy can have the same effect upon a family. What was once harmonious relationships become dissonant. Discord and strife fills the arena of life, resulting in bitterness.

Miriam experienced the effect of jealousy on her life when she spoke unkindly regarding her brother's marriage to the Cushite. The basis of Miriam's discontent was not the woman specifically, but the fear of losing power and authority. For forty years she had stood next to her brother. She had been a part of the decision-making process—in the inner circle. Now, she was afraid that Moses' wife would depose her. The result was an intense jealousy that resulted in her having to be disciplined strongly by God.

Family members have a choice; they can genuinely care for one another, or they can allow self-pity to run rampant in their lives, saying, "I'm not as good as my brother or sister." Or, they can even be outwardly jealous of another family member, resulting in God's discipline. Miriam stood the tallest when she put someone's welfare above her own. When Miriam genuinely was concerned, she had her most intense influence upon others. The questions brothers or sisters must answer today are, Where will I take my stand? Will it be in the area of self-pity and jealousy, or genuine concern?

SUGGESTIONS FOR LEADING THE BIBLE STUDY

From a study of the life of Miriam, youth can learn to relate to family members in such a way that God's will can be done in their individual lives as well as in their families.

Get Ready

Prepare the illustration for step 1. You will need a chalkboard and chalk or butcher paper and a felt-tip pen. Be prepared to lead the discussion called for in step 2. Prepare the short lecture for step 3. Follow the suggestions closely.

Lead the Bible Study

1. Instruct the youth to turn to Exodus 1:1 to 2:10 in their Bibles. Point them to the chalkboard or butcher paper where you have drawn the following illustration. Draw a large circle in the center of the paper or chalkboard. Write

66

Miriam in the center of the circle. Around the circle write *self, Moses, Aaron,* and *Mother.* Suggest to the group that they make note of the relationships of these people as they read the Exodus passage.

When they have finished reading the passage, ask the youth to list relationship characteristics between Miriam and the different people listed. Write their responses on the chalkboard or butcher paper.

2. Lead the youth in discussing some of the difficulties brothers and sisters will naturally experience. Then ask, What are some of the relationships that must be worked at most diligently by siblings? Finally, ask, What are some of the inherent blessings that come as the result of having brothers and/ or sisters?

3. Prepare and give a short lecture on Exodus 2:1-10. Include in the lecture how brothers and sisters can help their parents accomplish family goals and objectives. Help the youth to see how important Miriam was in accomplishing the family goal of preserving Moses' life. When you have finished the lecture ask, What if Miriam had not done as her mother asked?

4. Ask the youth to turn in their Bibles to Micah 6:4. Ask, What was Micah's point concerning the Exodus of Israel? (All three members of this family played a part in the Exodus. They worked together as a family to do God's will. Yet each of them performed specific functions within the will of God.) Help the youth to see that working together as a family, to accomplish God's will, is as important as each individual family member separately following God's plan.

5. Conclude by leading the group in prayer of thanksgiving for the privilege of being a part of a family. Include here the idea of the family of God. Ask each youth to commit himself to seeking to accomplish God's will personally and within his family group.

Moses:

Responding to God's Call

Exodus 3:1 to 4:31

David Self

Perhaps the greatest adventure in human history centers around Moses. The leading of an entire nation out of slavery to be established in a new location has fired the imaginations of not only Jews but also all people. Cecil B. deMille's *Ten Commandments* has brought this story to life and has acquainted most teenagers with a visualization of Moses.

How did a great man become great? Many youth are at a stage when simply dreaming dreams is not enough. They're beginning to have to make decisions that will help determine future paths of education, family, and life's work. The whole subject of God's will and God's call is a very relevant topic.

In this study, we'll explore the preparation and call of Moses. Through this study, perhaps God can speak to youth concerning the things he has in store for them.

Background of Moses

"Baby Moses in the basket" is one of the more touching stories in the Bible. However, the historical context that produced this story is tragic. Under the influence of Joseph, the Hebrew people had settled in the land of Goshen in Eastern Egypt. The Bible records that a pharaoh came into power who saw the Hebrews as a threat. A combination of their birthrate, strategic location, and prosperity caused the Egyptians to enslave the Israelites. In order to keep down the population, a decree was issued to slay every male Hebrew baby.

Thus, in order to save his life, Moses' parents hid him in the bulrushes of the river. There, in the providence of God, he was discovered by a princess who not only allowed him to live but also placed him back in his natural home! In this Hebrew home, Moses learned about God and his people. These early lessons had an important and lasting influence on Moses, which all the pagan influences on Pharaoh's court could not undo: "By faith Moses, when he had grown up, refused to be called the son of Pharaoh's daughter; choosing rather to endure ill-treatment with the people of God, than to enjoy the passing pleasures of sin'' (Heb. 11:24-25, NASB).

Many youth today can identify with having two sets of parents. The broken-home phenomenon in our country has forced many young people to glide in and out of different home settings and different family values. However, we could hardly imagine a greater contrast in homes than between that of the Pharaoh and the slave. As Moses was shifted back and forth, he had to adapt to great changes.

While learning of God from his Hebrew family, Moses was taught in the palace to worship the Pharaoh and the collection of Egyptian dieties.

Wealth can be very impressive to a young person. Imagine Moses having the run of the great palaces of Egypt all the while living in slave quarters. The slave mentality had been ground into the Hebrews for generations. On the one hand, Moses was surrounded by slaves, on the other by wealthy, free Egyptians.

''And Moses was educated in all the learning of the Egyptians, and he was a man of power in words and deeds'' (Acts 7:22, NASB). The young Moses had perhaps the finest education available in that ancient world. Egyptian scholars taught him things of which his kindred would never dream.

What struggles Moses must have endured! Should he believe the simple stories learned on his mother's knee; or should he trust in the apparent might of the Egyptians. Many nights Moses must have stared at the simple slave hut and compared it to the vaunted palaces of Pharaoh. If God was so powerful and loved his people so much, why were the Hebrews in slavery? During these formative years of his life, Moses could have made a clean break with his past and become a leader of Egypt. Yet those early lessons of the home gave him the strength to endure.

The Desert

The identity crisis of Moses is never more apparent than in Exodus 2:11-12 where his killing of an Egyptian taskmaster is recorded. Bound up in this story are hints of Moses' care for his people, hatred of injustice, and desire to liberate the Hebrews. Whatever good motives are revealed, the incident also shows recklessness and immaturity. As a result, he lost the respect of his own people (Ex. 2:14) and had to flee Egypt.

Moses' forty years in the Midianite desert tending sheep would seem to us to be utterly wasted years. However, from the changes we see in Moses' life, it is evident that God used this time to build on his early lessons and mold Moses into the man he needed. Many great figures of the Bible have spent a period of their lives in relative isolation with the Lord; witness Paul's three years in the

Arabian desert, Jesus' forty days in the wilderness, and John's exile on the isle of Patmos. Time is never wasted that is spent growing closer to God.

Emerging from the desert, Moses is revealed in the remainder of the Bible as a man with a mission; one who was more mature, confident, and patient to see God work his plan.

Call of Moses

Exodus 3 and 4 record the signal event of Moses' call on Mount Horeb. The burning-bush experience is in fact Moses' graduation experience from the years of training God had given him. By this time, Moses was well past the prime of his life; a man whose young dreams of liberation seem to have faded into forty years of wandering the Midianite desert. Yet God, in one bold stroke, showed Moses that his mission was only just beginning.

Reverence is the keynote of Moses' encounter with God. Moses was instructed to remove his sandals, and then he hid his face. Removing the sandals is obviously an act of reverence but perhaps also is a symbol of helplessness. In this desert setting, a person could do very little without proper footwear; God might have been underlining to his servant the fact of Moses' complete dependence on God. The educated, powerful prince of Egypt had at one time made an attempt in his own power to free his people and had utterly failed. Now God was saying, "Depend on me." True reverence comes when we realize our position in relationship to God's. Isaiah saw the Lord "sitting upon a throne, high and lifted up." Moses, too, recognized God's position and in reverent worship hid his face.

Revelation from God to Moses is the second aspect of this call. God chose as a medium the burning bush. Fire was recognized by most ancients as a symbol of deity: pure, majestic, and full of power. The bush burned but was not consumed. Moses could be used in a similar way for God's purpose, drawing on inner resources in a miraculous way. Finally, the bush was just an ordinary bush used by Jehovah in an extraordinary manner. Moses, at this point, was a simple ordinary shepherd about to be transformed by God into an extraordinary figure in history.

God's revelation was direct: "I will send you to Pharaoh, so that you may bring My people, the sons of Israel, out of Egypt" (Ex. 3:10, NASB). In this simple statement, God was fulfilling a promise made to Abraham long ago (Gen. 17:6 ff.); Abraham's seed would be a nation with kings, not slaves! In the passage, God acknowledged that the Hebrews' prayers had not gone unheard (Ex. 3:7). In character with all of God's callings, he chose a human servant. Note that God called Moses by name. Moses had been prepared in a special way to do a special mission, and now God was issuing instructions.

The response of Moses provides an interesting conclusion to this call. While Isaiah said, "Send me," and Jonah said, "Not me," Moses seems to have said, "Who, me?" Moses was under no delusions as to the difficulty of freeing the Hebrews. It is often God's hardest call that sends us back to a place of previous failure to try again. Moses openly confessed his doubts to God: The people would not respect him plus he was not an eloquent speaker. Again, God took an ordinary thing, Moses' staff, and used it to demonstrate extraordinary power. Don't expect to be excused when God calls you. God patiently listened to all Moses' excuses, taking time to answer each in its turn. God had trained Moses; he wanted Moses for this particular mission. Moses would do it now.

The call of Moses was reverence, revelation, and response. Each of these characteristics reveal something of God's call to each of his people. At this point in his life, Moses could look back and see how each aspect fitted into God's overall plan of training for him. In the next few years, his knowledge learned in the home, the palace, and the desert would all be vital to the freedom and existence of perhaps three million people. In God's work, hindsight is usually 20/20; Moses now had the confidence to face the future with that same faith.

Getting It Together

Several critical issues in the lives of youth are touched on in this study: self-identity, coping with a dual homelife, and God's preparation, call, and will.

Self-identity.—Who am I? The age-old question in all its simplicity came to life for Moses. In working out answers, Moses had to return to some basic lessons of the home: God, God's will, and personal loyalty. This problem in our culture is compounded by rootlessness. A teenager is often raised in a home espousing two religions, with no sense of history, purpose, or security. The lesson of Moses is that no matter the obstacles, we can find roots and identity in the eternal "I AM."

Dual Homes.—Many youth today are challenged to sort out various values (often conflicting) that face them from two sets of parents. This study may help some to begin facing issues that they have ignored. Each individual is ultimately responsible to choose beliefs and values for himself. We can help them see that the unchanging Word of God is an anchor which will provide security and authority.

God's preparations—call and will.—Adolescence is often a time of impatience, especially in relationship to God's revealed will. Youth often want it done now and grow restive at adults who seem to be treading water. Preparation is not an excuse for inaction. We need to be doing what we know to do at the same time God is preparing us for more.

God's call is an often misunderstood term. Youth tend to think strictly in terms of Christian vocational calling. We need to lead youth to understand that God uses his Word (rather than a modern burning bush) to call all Christians to live holy lives, to pray, to study, to witness, to give, and so forth. In addition, God has special callings for each of us if we remain sensitive to his urging.

God's will is bound closely with the idea of call. God reveals his will for us in his Word. Unfortunately we tend to think of God's will as spiritual "hide and seek." God's will is not a guessing game but a matter of consistently following him day by day and saying yes to his revealed will.

Dwight L. Moody once said that there are three classes of people: the wills, the won'ts, and the can'ts. The first accomplish everything. The second oppose everything. The third fail at everything.

Despite all his early struggles, Moses replied, "I will." With that simple decision, he walked down the path of history, blazing new trails that still inspire us today. Moses allowed God to do great things through him; can God expect less of us?

SUGGESTIONS FOR LEADING THE BIBLE STUDY

From a study of an experience in the life of Moses, youth can learn to make a proper response to God's call.

Get Ready

You will need pencils and paper for step 1. Prepare the short lecture for step 2. Don't forget the youth's response to the lecture makes it effective. Youth will need their Bibles, a pencil, and paper for step 3.

Lead Bible Study

1. As youth arrive, give each a pencil and a sheet of paper. Instruct them to draw two horizontal lines, labeling one *physical* and the other *spiritual*. On the physical line mark *birth* at the left end and *death* at the right end. In proportional scale, have each youth to mark and label the following points on the line (some will have to be guesstimates). First girl or boyfriend, graduation from high school, college, marriage, children, retirement, and so forth.

On the spiritual line, mark *salvation* at the left end and *image of Christ* at the right end. Intervening marks might include baptism, special decisions, or spiritual highlights.

Ask: How does your physical journey compare to your spiritual one? If our ultimate goal, spiritually, is to be conformed to the image of Christ, how are you progressing?

Help the youth see that God has a plan for our lives that coordinates the physical and spiritual rather than separates them. Our challenge in life is to allow God to work through us to accomplish his plan in our lives.

2. Prepare a lecture to give the youth an understanding of the life of Moses up to the time of the burning bush. Remember that the youth will have heard of "Baby Moses in the basket" many times. Help them see God's leading in Moses' education by Egypt and his family. Use the material up to "Call of Moses" to prepare your lecture. Keep the lecture short and interesting. Ask the youth to listen for the most important thing that prepared Moses for God's call (his personal relationship with God). When you finish your lecture, ask the youth for their response.

3. Ask the youth to read silently Exodus 3:1-10 and to write a brief paraphrase of the story in a modern setting. Allow youth to share the stories with each other, and ask for volunteers to read some aloud. You may wish to ask the youth to pair off to share their stories. Then ask a few to share with the entire group.

4. Ask some of the youth to share one incident in the life of Moses that relates the most to them. How did Moses act in the situation? How should we react?

Nehemiah:

Getting the Job Done

Nehemiah 1 to 6

David Self

My father served in the Seabee's during World War II. The motto of this naval construction group is, "Can do!" What a positive statement of accomplishment! A brief reading of Nehemiah will allow you to see that Nehemiah had the "can do" spirit.

Having passed through the "me generation" of the seventies, teenagers are faced with conflicting values. Is it right to give up personal comfort for the good of others? Are there virtues in hard work? Are there still accomplishments for which one should sacrifice?

This study of Nehemiah 1—6 gives a refreshing look at some old-fashioned values in God's Word.

Work comes in all shapes and sizes. A teenager is often asked to do individual work (carry out the trash), partnership work (go visit this absentee together), and group work (please help our Youth group raise money for a mission project). It is often at the point of work that we're able to see just what a teen is "made out of." It is a depressing fact that sometimes a seemingly spiritual, gung ho Christian teenager is lazy and noncommittal about doing needed work for the benefit of others.

Work According to Nehemiah

Nehemiah provides an interesting look at steps needed to see a major task accomplished. Obviously, not all these steps are applicable to most mundane chores; yet, taken as a whole they provide a model for taking on many physical and/or spiritual challenges.

Step 1, know the reason.—The Book of Nehemiah opens with a plaintive description of the sad state of affairs in Jerusalem. At this time Nehemiah was a highly placed official (cupbearer) in the court of Artaxerxes, king of the Persian empire. Since the time of Cyrus, nearly a century earlier, Jews had been permitted to return to Jerusalem from Exile. Therefore, Nehemiah was still in Susa, the capitol, by choice. The tale told by the visiting Jews from Judah was, to say the least, disturbing to Nehemiah. "The survivors . . . are in great trouble and shame; the wall of Jerusalem is broken down and its gates are destroyed by fire" (Neh. 1:3, RSV).

The walls of a city provided physical security from attack. With walls broken and gates burned, Jerusalem lay open to attack and plunder from any marauding bands. The walls also symbolized the prestige and might of a city in the ancient world. The higher and thicker the walls, the more powerful, generally, was the city. So, Jerusalem was in a state of physical danger and emotional shame. No wonder Nehemiah was so upset that he fasted and mourned for days!

At the same time, a clear goal began to form in Nehemiah's mind: The walls must be rebuilt! The task was clear; the reasons for it, evident. Nehemiah approached his job with a clear understanding of its necessity and importance. Unfortunately, sometimes youth are asked to do things both at home and church with no reasons given and no ultimate goal established! Youth as well as adults need to know the reason for tasks.

Step 2, pray.—The intercessory prayer of Nehemiah is recorded in 1:5-11. Several interesting facets come to light from his prayer. First of all, the prayer shows upon whom Nehemiah depended to accomplish things. A rich civil servant might have been expected to do something immediately; perhaps a relief offering sent to Jerusalem would have been in order. But, Nehemiah turned to God first. Also, it may be supposed that Nehemiah did not immediately understand that God had chosen him to do the task. But, by his willingness to pray and seek God's will, he was convicted to do it. Let us never simply pray for missions, pray for the poor, or pray for group unity without being willing to do something about them. Finally, Nehemiah's prayer emphasized his people's sin but recalled God's promises. The cupbearer had no puffed up conception of his own importance but rather trusted in God's faithfulness to keep his word. Through prayer Nehemiah received a new look at the rebuilding of the walls. To paraphrase a popular saying, prayer changes us.

Step 3, be commited.—Once Nehemiah clearly visualized the goal and received God's instructions through prayer, he was unswerving in his commitment. Note what Nehemiah had to immediately give up in order to build the walls of Jerusalem. In the space of six chapters, we see Nehemiah go from the king's chambers, surrounded by luxury, to the walls of Jerusalem and the hardest of manual labor. In the ancient world, Nehemiah was what you might call "set for life" in Susa. Located in the center of power, with all the creature comforts one might want, Nehemiah was as high on the pinnacle of success as he could ever expect to go. One might understand if he had wanted to retire in luxury at Susa. On the other hand, who would have ever heard of Nehemiah had he chosen to do so?

Someone once said that the great things in life are accomplished by lop-sided people. This is to say, people who will commit body and soul to a narrow field of endeavor will accomplish more in a shorter time when people who try to do everything for everyone. Often youth spread themselves so thin between umpteen organizations at school and myriads of activities at church that they accomplish little for anyone. Nehemiah was committed to one goal at a time: build the walls!

Step 4, count the cost.—Nehemiah was not one for a lot of talk. Often we hear big plans from people but see little if any production. Nehemiah was in Jerusalem three days before he told anyone about the walls! During this time he surveyed, planned, and obtained a good idea of just what it would take to build the walls.

Too often a job is left unfinished because someone wouldn't face reality. Nehemiah found a bleak scene at Jerusalem. But rather than discouraging him, his inspection simply confirmed the need for the job to be done.

Step 5, involve people.—A good lesson is available here for Youth leaders as well as youth. When Nehemiah had all his facts together, he took them before the rulers of Jerusalem (2:17). Very clearly and succinctly he described the problem and God's solution to it. He received his answer, "Let us rise up and build." When God's people are clearly faced with the facts, they normally respond positively to doing his work.

A simple affirmation to do the work was not enough; good intentions don't build walls. Chapter 3 itemizes the simple yet well-conceived plan for rebuilding the walls and gates. Each group of workmen was responsible for a given stretch of construction. Assignments were not equal, but all worked together. Nehemiah 3:5 hints that some refused to work, but no one else used this as an excuse not to do his part.

Step 6, work hard.—There are no easy ways to do some things. A few hours spent in laying block will tend to confirm this opinion. Rebuilding the wall was heavy, manual labor performed under a hot Judean sun. The work was contin-uous, sunup to sundown. When the threat of attack came, the workman liter-ally had a weapon in one hand, ready to fight at a moment's notice. Something of the relentlessness of all this can be seen in 4:23, "None of us put off our clothes, saving that everyone put them off for washing." Nehemiah and his band of guards, were on call twenty-four hours a day for emergency attacks.

Some people are discouraged by hard work. Many would rather spend time talking about it. Nehemiah, though, was a doer; he led his people by his own example.

Step 7, expect opposition.—Especially in spiritual projects, expect opposi-tion. Satan is not content to let gains come easily. Notice the progression of opposition to Nehemiah:

Scorn (4:1-4): The enemy at first tried to discourage the Jews by mocking them. "The wall is not important; it will take too long to build; it'll never last!" Often in our spiritual lives the devil can discourage us with simple words. Misunderstandings, envy, or a casual remark are all that's needed to stop our work. Nehemiah, however, used a sticks-and-stones philosophy and kept right on working.

Physical threats (4:4-8): As the walls kept rising, the enemies decided to take more direct action. Nehemiah established a system of warning stations and a plan of defense. Though these measures compounded the work and hampered it, the work never ceased. When faced with great obstacles, sometimes the work must slow down, but don't let a good project stop due to obstacles.

Talk rather than work (6:1-2): Nehemiah's enemies tried yet another strategy to divert his course. "If we can just sit down and talk about this, I'm sure we can work something out." Nehemiah saw this for the plot it was and refused to leave the city.

How much easier it is to talk about something than it is to do something about it! One housewife remarked to another, "I wish housework were like committee work; then we could talk about it instead of doing it."

Rumors (6:6): "It is reported . . ." How simple but vicious gossip is! The enemies in this instance tried to threaten Nehemiah by spreading tales of rebellion. Nehemiah wisely dismissed it for the false gossip it was.

Many youth are halted in their spiritual journeys by false rumors and gossip. It's often easier to believe and spread gossip than it is to check the accuracy of a statement. Remember it takes two to spread rumors: one to tell and one to listen. Don't be used to hurt someone by doing either!

False friends (6:12): Nehemiah and his work were finally threatened from inside by someone hired to kill him. This false prophet claimed to be a friend and even a messenger from God. When all attacks from the outside had failed, the enemy tried to cause problems from within.

It is a shocking thing to have a supposed friend betray you. Teenagers seeking belonging and security can feel terribly betrayed by false friends. Remember: a friend who tries to cause you hurt was never a true friend at all. Against all opposition, Nehemiah held to his sense of purpose.

Step 8, see it through.—In 6:15 we read the triumphant words, "So the wall was completed . . . in fifty-two days" (NASB). For almost two months Nehemiah and his band had worked hard, slept little, and fought off discouragement and the enemy. But now that glorious word could be said, *finished*! All the deprivations of the past fifty-two days seemed worthwhile.

Perhaps the most important quality of any major project is endurance, seeing the project through to completion. Many of our youth need to see that the Christian life is more a long-distance run than a sprint. Youth will see progress if they simply keep moving forward.

Getting It Together

Nehemiah stands tall in history as an example of single-mindedness and hard work. Seldom will we have to work under the conditions and pressure of his day. Yet, many of the approaches he took can apply to modern projects, both physical and spiritual.

Jesus had much to say about service and servanthood. At the heart of our Christian self-image should be a willing servant. Proper service not only involves the attitudes of humility and love but also results in constructive things being done for others.

This study of Nehemiah should not major on work for the joy of work. But, rather, emphasis should be placed on accomplishment, helping others, and self-sacrifice for the common good.

SUGGESTIONS FOR LEADING THE BIBLE STUDY

From a study of the life of Nehemiah, youth can learn that meaningful work can help them accomplish goals, help others, and be a means of self-sacrifice.

Get Ready

Be prepared to give clear instructions for playing the "Who am I?" game in step 1. Also make provision for your being Nehemiah. Prepare the eight posters for step 2. You will also need to prepare the lecture for step 2.

Lead Bible Study

Play a question/answer game "Who am I?" Allow several youth to pretend to be major Bible personalities, and let the other youth ask questions that require yes-or-no answers. After each answer is given, the youth who asked the question may hazard a guess as to the identity of the person. If you want to keep score, allow only one guess per person per personality and let point value decline as the number of questions increases.

While interest is still high, tell the youth that you will be one last personality (Nehemiah). If you choose not to play the role yourself, be sure to pick someone in advance who can study the life of Nehemiah. When Nehemiah has been correctly identified, briefly review the facts about him the youth have uncovered and move into the study.

Prepare in advance eight small posters with the eight steps outlined under "Work According to Nehemiah." Prepare a lecture using these eight steps as your points. As you discuss each in turn, give the poster for that step to a different youth. At the conclusion of the study, challenge the youth with posters to correctly align themselves in the order that you covered the points. (In larger groups, two sets of posters of different colors may be divided between two teams for a race to see who can first line up correctly at the conclusion of the material.)

Ask youth what step gives them the most trouble in getting things done. Have them stand with the youth holding the poster for the step they have chosen. Instruct all eight groups to prepare a two-to-three minute role play showing the difficulty they have with their step. Ask them to use a modern situation to show the difficulty and how to overcome the difficulty. After each group performs, briefly discuss the results.

Paul:

A New Beginning (New Year's)

2 Corinthians 5:17-21

Kathryn Griffin

There was a protest from the back of the crowd. The voice was like the stampeding of horses on the parched earth. It rumbled over the heads of his countrymen and trailed off into the air like an echo. "Nothing is free these days," the man said cynically.

"I assure you," the speaker continued, "it has been bought and paid for. It is a gift."

"Ha!" the voice exploded. Then the man spat on the ground. A gift, indeed! How long had it been since anyone had offered him a gift? Twenty years? Gifts were for children—a coin, a trinket, a soft ball of wool with the smell of the out-of-doors upon it. Gifts were for brides. Or the wealthy. Perhaps the wealthy could give gifts to each other. They had nothing else to do.

It had been a hard year for Antonius, and the next was likely to be worse. Forty percent it was costing him in taxes. And another 5 percent he must pay for the privilege of operating his business.

Everything had its price. Peace. Roads. Travel. Protection. Even religion. Nothing was free.

"I don't believe you," he said. It wasn't that he wouldn't have liked to.

The speaker was not discouraged. He had met folk like Antonius before. His heart went out to them. "You will be a brand new person," he always told them, and most of them were impressed. They would like to be new people. They would like to start all over again and have another chance at life.

That was what the speaker was offering them—new life.

Antonius rested his eyes on the shadow of the hills against the sky and fought with his emotions. He could not afford to turn soft. He must keep up his front. He must plod on. He must do what was expected of him. People were depending on him.

But new life? Another man altogether? The idea washed over his soul like a breeze from off the sea. It was fresh and pure. It was inordinately calming. It tugged at the old ways and promised to blow them away.

Ah, how he would like to believe! A new creature—old things passed away—a new mind, a new heart—love in place of hate. To dream again, to have plans for his life, to believe his fellowman, to substitute righteousness and purity of motives for the graft, violence, and degradation that had swept over his soul: what person in the crowd that day or throughout the whole country who would not give up an arm or a leg for such a chance?

"Therefore if any man be in Christ, he is a new creature: old things are passed away; behold, all things are become new" (2 Cor. 5:17).

The words had a beauty to them.

"All things are of God, who hath reconciled us to himself by Jesus Christ, and hath given to us the ministry of reconciliation" (2 Cor. 5:18).

The tears streamed down Antonius' face. A peacemaker. If he accepted God's peace for himself, he would in turn be a peacemaker. It was not a demand. It was a desire that would follow naturally, like the night on the heels of the day, the calm after the storm, springtime after winter.

"God was in Christ, reconciling the world unto himself, not imputing their trespasses unto them; and hath committed unto us the word of reconciliation. Now then we are ambassadors for Christ, as though God did beseech you by us: we pray you in Christ's stead, be ye reconciled to God. For he hath made him to be sin for us, who knew no sin; that we might be made the righteousness of God in him" (2 Cor. 5:19-21).

It was too marvelous. God became a man? And so that people like Antonius could better understand him? God really cared that much? He wanted to be a part of human life?

What a strange kind of God he was: not vindictive and unpredictable and full of plans for humanity's undoing. He didn't, as a matter of fact, hold people's sins against them. His own Son volunteered to take the blame, and in the sacrificing of himself he had somehow mysteriously swept away the barriers between people and God. He had enabled all people to become their own priests.

Antonius a priest? He laughed. He laughed out loud. It was good to be laughing. It rumbled and rolled and got completely away from him! He was happy! How long had it been since he had been so happy? He was going to be a new man—a new creature in Christ Jesus! He had never heard such wonderful news.

He was going home to tell Claudia.

Old days, old ways, last year, other years, the old life: they were all behind him now. He would remember them no more, just as God would remember them no more. He had never ever felt so good.

> Give me a day without a past.
> Just one new day: that's all I ask—

A day that has no prior claims,
A day that's made for lofty aims.

Give me a day that's bright and clear:
No fog or clouds to mar the cheer.
I need a day that's mine to use:
A day for doing what I choose.

Paul the apostle was the bearer of good news. In Christ there is no yesterday, he said. Every day is new and unspotted. Every day is a new beginning.

What glorious news that was to people whose lives were hopelessly en-
tangled in sin and guilt. What wonderful news it is to us for the same reason.
We are not prisoners of our guilt. The past need not condemn us. In Christ we
are not haunted by yesterday's mistakes and inadequacies. We learn from
them, but we do not torture ourselves with the memories of them.

What can we learn from the brilliant and gifted Paul about new beginnings? What would he be likely to say to us about a brand-new year?

Take Inventory

"Whereupon, O king Agrippa, I was not disobedient unto the heavenly
vision, but shewed first unto them of Damascus, and at Jerusalem, and
throughout all the coasts of Judaea, and then to the Gentiles, that they should
repent and turn to God, and do works meet for repentance" (Acts 26:19-20).

"If any other man thinketh that he hath whereof he might trust in the
flesh, I more: Circumcised the eighth day, of the stock of Israel, of the tribe of
Benjamin, an Hebrew of the Hebrews; as touching the law, a Pharisee; Concerning zeal, persecuting the church; touching the righteousness which is in
the law, blameless" (Phil. 3:4-6).

"Those things, which ye have both learned, and received, and heard, and
seen in me, do" (Phil. 4:9).

"For that which I do I allow not: for what I would, that do I not; but
what I hate, that do I. . . . For the good that I would I do not: but the evil
which I would not, that I do" (Rom. 7:15,19).

"I am debtor both to the Greeks, and to the Barbarians; both to the wise,
and to the unwise" (Rom. 1:14).

"For so hath the Lord commanded us, saying, I have set thee to be a light
of the Gentiles" (Acts 13:47).

"I have fought a good fight, I have finished my course, I have kept the
faith" (2 Tim. 4:7).

Paul was keenly aware of both his good and bad points. He acknowledged his human tendencies, his weaknesses and insufficiencies. He didn't try to pretend they weren't there. Nor was he oblivious to his assets: the keen mind he had been endowed with, his rare insights, and his enormous capacity for love and forgiveness. He recognized and showed appreciation for the forces and the people who had contributed to his life. He had had an excellent education. He had been trained in the Law. He was a citizen of the world and had learned from and been influenced by the Greek culture, the Hebrews who were his people, the Romans with whom he shared citizenship, and the vast throngs of non-Jewish, non-Christian people who both encouraged him by their attentiveness and perfected his faith by their opposition and persecution. He followed Christ so closely and so faithfully that he was able to tell others to follow his example. Then, near the end of his life, he was able to say, in essence, "I have done a good job of what I set out to do. I have been faithful to my calling." Always, he gave credit to God for who he was.

Paul took inventory frequently. He knew himself quite well. We would do well to do the same.

Forget the Past

"Forgetting those things which are behind, and reaching forth unto those things which are before, I press toward the mark for the prize of the high calling of God in Christ Jesus" (Phil. 3:13-14).

All through his life, Paul had reason both to brag about and to be haunted by his past. He did neither.

Before he became a Christian, Paul persecuted the Christians. The memory could have incapacitated him. Instead, for the rest of his life, he treated Christians everywhere like his own children. He loved them, instructed them, chided them, forgave them, understood them, and took pride in them.

It isn't easy to do an about-face. It is the natural thing to be embarrassed and intimidated by those we have wronged. We want to hide from the reminders of our mistakes. Paul rose above this human tendency. With enormous courage and determination, he wrenched himself from the past and kept his face turned toward the future. Because God was able to forgive Paul and to see his unusual possibilities, Paul became able to forgive himself. He had to get rid of the shackles of self-incrimination before he could speak to others of the marvels of freedom.

As he traveled from city to city and continent to continent, Paul experienced every conceivable kind of hardship. It would have been understandable if he had said, "Enough is enough," and let somebody else take over after he had done his share. But Paul's threshold of pain was very high. He kept on taking abuses, returning to the places where they had been meted out, and did not allow them to overshadow his joys. Yesterday's hardships did not destroy his present or his future.

Remember to Say Thanks

"I thank my God upon every remembrance of you" (Phil. 1:3). "Your care of me hath flourished again" (Phil. 4:10). "Giving thanks to God and the Father by him" (Col. 3:17). "For I have learned, in whatsoever state I am, therewith to be content" (Phil. 4:11). "Thanks be unto God for his unspeakable gift" (2 Cor. 9:15). "Greet Priscilla and Aquila . . . who have for my life laid down their own necks" (Rom. 16:3-4).

From Paul we learn to be grateful. He was gracious toward those who had helped him. He constantly gave thanks to God for the gift of salvation and the kind of life he made available. Paul was thankful even for the hardships that made him a better person. The ability to express thanks graciously may be cultivated by all.

Set Goals

A goal is a resolution, either expressed orally or decided on privately. Here are some New Year's resolutions we might learn from Paul:

"Glorify God in your body, and in your spirit" (1 Cor. 6:20).

"Let no man despise thy youth: but be thou an example of the believers, in word, in conversation, in charity, in spirit, in faith, in purity" (1 Tim. 4:12).

"Neglect not the gift that is in thee" (1 Tim. 4:14a).

"Henceforth be no more children, tossed to and fro" (Eph. 4:14).

"Submitting yourselves one to another in the fear of God" (Eph. 5:21).

"Be kindly affectioned one to another" (Rom. 12:10).

"Let every soul be subject unto the higher powers" (Rom. 13:1).

"We then that are strong ought to bear the infirmities of the weak, and not to please ourselves" (Rom. 15:1).

"Quench not the Spirit" (1 Thess. 5:19).

SUGGESTIONS FOR LEADING THE BIBLE STUDY

From a study of portions of the life of Paul, youth can learn to make a new commitment that will affect the new year.

Get Ready

Step 1 calls for a poem to be written on the chalkboard. You may consider newsprint if your chalkboard is small. Step 3 also calls for the use of the chalkboard. You will need a pencil and paper for each youth in step 4.

Lead Bible Study

1. On a chalkboard write the poem on pages 81-82. Lead the youth to point out ways in which the poem is both Christian and self-centered in content.

2. Call on various youths to read a paragraph each in the fictional story of Antonius and to list some of the major teachings of Paul that are reflected in the story. (Salvation is a gift. Christians become new people through belief in God. Christians are reconcilers, ambassadors, and priests. Forgiveness is essential in and to the Christian life.)

3. Assign as many of the Scripture passages as is feasible. As youth make suggestions, list on the chalkboard or other medium what we learn from Paul about new beginnings.

4. Lead youth to make written self-inventories, listing good points which need to be further strengthened and developed, bad points which need to be eliminated altogether or converted to strengths, specific ways in which they have grown throughout the preceeding year, and at least five people who have contributed significantly to their lives in recent days. Call for a voluntary sharing of inventories by categories (all the good points first, then the bad, the marks of growth, and, finally, contributions).

5. Lead youth to express through sentence prayers or an add-a-line group prayer (a paper passed around the circle and youth write a line apiece) at least one New Year's resolution.

Peter:

Overcoming Prejudice

Acts 10:1-48

Forrest W. Jackson

Peter was just like most of us. He liked people like himself. He had been taught that way. Peter associated with people who basically believed like he did. It wasn't that Peter hated Gentiles. He just didn't have anything to do with them.

However, God was in the process of changing Peter to be like Jesus. Many youth are followers of Jesus. They know Jesus Christ by personal faith. They are in the process of being changed to be like their Lord in attitude and deed.

God Revealed Himself to Cornelius (vv. 1-8)

Cornelius was a "centurion" (v. 1). He was the leader of one hundred Roman soldiers. Centurions were the backbone of the Roman army, similar to our sergeants. Centurions were usually very dependable men.

Cornelius was also a very "religious man" (v. 2, NEB). This probably meant that he was a person who believed in *Yahweh,* the God of the Jews. In keeping with his faith in *Yahweh,* Cornelius did many good things for people (probably mostly Jews) and prayed regularly.

One day Cornelius saw an angel in a vision. The angel said, "And now send to Joppa for a man named Simon, also called Peter: he is lodging with another Simon, a tanner, whose house is by the sea" (v. 6, NEB). After the vision was over, Cornelius sent two of his slaves and a trusted soldier to get Peter. (The manuscripts differ on how many were sent by Cornelius.) God had prepared Cornelius to receive the gospel.

God Gave Peter a Special Vision (vv. 9-16)

God's hardest work was with Peter, the Christian. Too often it's that way. God can get people ready to hear the gospel easier than he can get Christian messengers to take the gospel to them. This is especially true where prejudice is present. And Peter was prejudiced against Gentiles.

Peter went to the roof of the house to pray. Often that was also the place to catch whatever breeze was blowing. He became hungry and "fell into a trance" (v. 10, NEB). God had begun to prepare Peter to receive Cornelius' messengers.

"A great sheet of sail-cloth" (v. 11, NEB) was let down out of heaven. It was filled with all kinds of animals. Jews were allowed to eat animals declared to be ritually clean in their law but were forbidden to eat unclean animals. Since the animals were all together in the sheet, all of them were considered unclean by the law. When God told Peter to kill one of the animals and eat it, Peter refused. (Cornelius obeyed; Peter disobeyed.) This was repeated three times. Then the vision ended.

Each time Peter refused to obey, God said, "It is not for you to call profane what God counts clean" (v. 15, NEB). Peter couldn't understand what God was trying to say to him. God said in effect, "Peter, nothing that I have created is unclean." This was a reminder that everything God created was good (see Gen. 1). This may also have been a reminder of Jesus' words (see Mark 7:1-23). Jesus had rejected the Jewish food taboos when he said, " 'Nothing that goes into a man from outside can defile him; no, it is the things that come out of him that defile a man.' . . . Thus he declared all foods clean" (Mark 7:15,19, NEB). God was trying to get Peter to understand that he was not to be prejudiced against Gentiles or any person God created.

God Put It Together for Peter (vv. 17-23)

Have you ever noticed God's timing in the Bible? Here is an excellent example of how God works. Peter woke up wondering what the vision meant. Just as the question entered his mind, he heard a voice saying, "Is there a guest here by the name of Simon Peter?" (v. 18, TEV). Just as Peter heard this call from the front gate, the Spirit let him know that these men were looking for him. The Spirit also indicated that Peter was to go with them, for God has sent them. The Greek word can mean "nothing doubting" or "making no distinction" (v. 20). In this context, the latter seems better. When Peter got to the gate, there stood a Roman Gentile and two slaves.

Being a country boy, Peter said something like, "What can I do for ya?" The soldier told Peter the story of the vision of Cornelius. He ended by telling Peter that God told Cornelius to send for him. Peter was to go and preach the gospel of Jesus Christ. He was a special witness of Jesus' life, death, and resurrection.

Peter invited them to spend the night there. It was an extraordinary move. No self-respecting Jew would have done it. But a Christian Jew would, especially if God had just challenged his prejudice against Gentiles.

The next day Peter and "some members of the congregation at Joppa"

(v. 23, NEB) made the trip to the home of Cornelius. Luke doesn't say why these believers went along. It seems likely that Peter invited them to go. How else could they have known about the trip? Cornelius sent only for Peter. Could it be that Peter was having a problem with peer pressure? Could he have wanted some friends to verify what happened at the Gentile's house? Youth can certainly identify with Peter at this point. Going against the beliefs of the peer group is difficult for youth, if not impossible.

Peter Obeyed God (vv. 24-33)

Whatever struggle Peter may have had, he obeyed God. When Peter was sure that God wanted him to go, he went. It was something new for Peter. He wasn't sure of himself. His heart said go, but his gut said no. That's the way it is when a person seeks to change his prejudices. He must do what is right when his insides rebel against it. Youth need to learn this lesson. They are faced with prejudice every day.

When Peter arrived, Cornelius fell at his feet to worship him. What would you have done if an angel of God told you to send for someone? Peter must be a person to reverence. Right? Wrong! Peter immediately got Cornelius on his feet and refused to be anything but a human being (vv. 25-26).

Peter seemed bound to remind these Gentiles that it was unlawful for him to be with them. (Or was this for the Jewish Christians he had brought along?) However, Peter didn't stop there. He told them God had shown him that he was not to treat Gentiles as unclean. Peter had learned what God showed him in the vision. Prejudice can have no place in Christianity. Jesus is the Savior of all people. Only those who will not believe are excluded.

Then Peter asked what seems to be a stupid question. "Why did you send for me?" (v. 29, TEV). Could it be that Peter still could not realize that the gospel of Jesus Christ was for these Gentiles? Peter's question must have been something like an evangelist going to a revival meeting and asking, "Why did you send for me?" In other circumstances, the answer would be obvious. Prejudice clouds minds, even liberated minds. For whatever the reason, Cornelius had to tell Peter his story for the second time. (The soldier had already told it once in verse 22). Cornelius seemed to be a little exasperated (v. 33). He must have said, "For godness sakes tell us what you know."

Peter Preached the Gospel (vv. 34-43)

These verses give a glimpse of apostolic preaching. Peter's opening statement was aimed at the life situation facing him. "I now realize that it is true that God treats everyone on the same basis. Whoever fears him and does what is right is acceptable to him, no matter what race he belongs to" (vv. 34-35,

TEV). In this context "whoever fears him" would be better translated "whoever has reverence for him." Peter was speaking of faith. Christians need to live by these two verses of Scripture.

Peter then spoke of God sending Jesus to the people of Israel. He mentioned John and his baptism. He spoke of the Holy Spirit giving Jesus power. Peter included Jesus' doing good and defeating the devil. Then Peter preached the cross and the resurrection of Jesus. He claimed to be a personal witness of Jesus' resurrection. Next Peter said that Jesus commanded all who were witnesses to preach this good news to all who would listen. Finally, Peter said that Jesus was the one the prophets of Israel had spoken of. "Everyone who trusts in him receives forgiveness of sins through his name" (v. 43, NEB).

The Holy Spirit Interrupted Peter's Sermon (vv. 44-48)

Evidently each person who heard Peter's sermon exercised personal faith in Jesus and wanted the forgiveness of sin because the Holy Spirit "came upon all who were listening to the message" (v. 44, NEB). The evidence that the Holy Spirit had entered these Gentiles was similar to Pentecost. Some have seen this chapter of Acts as the "Gentile Pentecost." Could God have used this spectacular means so there would be no doubt that Gentiles were included in the kingdom of God? Only faith in Christ is required to be a Christian. All other human distinctions and requirements must be laid aside.

God often surprises Christians. "The Jewish believers who had come from Joppa with Peter were amazed that God had poured out his gift of the Holy Spirit on the Gentiles also" (v. 45, TEV). Notice that God reversed the usual order. Usually in the New Testament the order is faith, baptism, and the gift of the Spirit. Here it is faith, the gift of the Holy Spirit, and then baptism.

God still surprises us with his acceptance of people we reject. Youth are not immune from labeling other people as "not acceptable." They need to hear again the words of this passage. James said it more plainly, "But if you treat people according to their outward appearance, you are guilty of sin" (2:9, TEV).

Since the Holy Spirit had saved and accepted Cornelius and the other Gentiles, Peter felt no Christian could object to their Christian baptism (see however 11:2-3). "So he ordered them to be baptized in the name of Jesus Christ" (v. 48, TEV). Then Peter stayed "a few days" and probably instructed the Gentile believers in the ethics of Christian living.

There are at least three lessons we need to learn from this experience of Peter. (1) Prejudice is sin. God's revelation to us is to forsake prejudice. (2) God's actions show his equal acceptance of every person who has faith in

Christ. If we are "in Christ," we are also "in each other." (3) God's acceptance of us while we are sinners, should remind us to share God's grace-gospel with every person.

SUGGESTIONS FOR LEADING BIBLE STUDY

From a study of the life of Peter, youth can learn that prejudice is sin and overcome it.

Get Ready

Have a large piece of butcher paper ready for the focal wall. Also have masking tape or some means for attaching the butcher paper to the wall. Several felt-tip pens will be necessary for step 1. See step 2 for a suggested question/answer sheet you will have to prepare. Pencils will also be needed. Read step 2 carefully for suggestions for the needed lecture. You will need pencils and paper for step 3. For step 5 you will need chalk and a chalkboard.

Lead Bible Study

1. Attach a piece of butcher paper to your focal wall. With a felt-tip pen, write the words *Prejudice Is* . . . in fairly large letters on the paper. Have several felt-tip pens available. As youth enter the room, ask each of them to complete the sentence in their own words on the paper. (Possible answers: putting people down, feeling superior to others, sin, and excluding people from your group.)

2. Give each youth a pencil and the question/answer sheets you prepared. You may wish to use the following examples. (1) Who was Cornelius? (2) Why did God do something special for Cornelius? (3) What did God ask Cornelius to do? (4) Why did God have to show Peter a vision? (5) How was Peter prejudiced? (6) Why did Peter refuse to kill an animal and eat when God told him to? (7) How did God's timing of the soldier's arrival help Peter understand? (8) What was remarkable about Peter's asking the soldier and slaves to spend the night? (9) Why did Peter ask some Christians from Joppa to go with him? (10) In what way was Peter dealing with peer pressure? (Make your question/answer sheet in such a way that the youth can write the answers immediately following the questions.)

Give the lecture you have prepared. The lecture should cover Acts 10:1-23. Use the background material included under the headings "God Revealed Himself to Cornelius (vv. 1-8)," "God Gave Peter a Special Vision (vv. 9-16)," and "God Put It Together for Peter (vv. 17-23)." Also be sure to bring out the answers to the questions on the "question/answer sheets" in your lecture. Add whatever further insights you wish to get across to your youth.

3. Ask the youth to read Acts 10:24-43 in their Bibles. Give them pencils and paper. (They could use the back of the question/answer sheets.) Ask them to outline Peter's sermon. Tell them to find the introduction and main points of the sermon (vv. 34-43). Example: Introduction (vv. 34-35), (1) God sent Jesus to Israel to preach good news to everyone (vv. 36-37), (2) God anointed Jesus with the Holy Spirit and power (v. 38), (3) Jesus went about doing good and healing those oppressed by the devil (v. 38), (4) Jesus died on the tree (cross) (v. 39), (5) God resurrected Jesus from the dead and I saw him alive (vv. 40-41), (6) Jesus commanded us to preach this good news, (7) the Old Testament prophets bear witness to Jesus, and everyone who puts personal faith in Jesus will be forgiven for his sins. (Don't be afraid to accept variations of this outline.)

Call for several youth to share their understanding of Peter's outline. Other youth may fill in their outline where they differ.

4. Ask, Why didn't Peter have a conclusion to his sermon? If they don't know, ask them to read verses 44-48 in their Bibles. Referring to verse 45, ask, Why were the Jewish Christians surprised at the Holy Spirit's coming upon these Gentiles? (They thought he would only be given to the Jews.)

5. Divide your youth into groups of three. Ask each group to decide how youth today are prejudiced in ways similar to Peter. Then ask them to decide what God would like them to do about these prejudices. Give them a few minutes for discussion. Call for reports. Put their answers to the first question on the chalkboard or write them on the *Prejudice Is* . . . paper. Hopefully, their answer to the second question will be to ask God's forgiveness and to overcome their prejudices.

Close with prayer, asking God's help to your youth to deal with prejudice with courage like Peter's.

Philip:

Profile of a Personal Witness

Acts 8:26-40

David Self

Introduce the study on Philip by discussing the fact that many people are not experiencing God's love. However, we have the privilege and the responsibility of sharing his love with them. Philip, the witnessing deacon, is an excellent example of a person who knew God's love and was willing to share it.

Acts 8:26-40 records the account of Philip witnessing to the Ethiopian eunuch. Let's look at three questions: Who was Philip? Who was the Ethiopian, and what were they doing together?

Philip

First of all, don't get this Philip confused with the disciple Philip. Philip is first mentioned in Acts 6:5. A look at his qualifications may give us insight into some prerequisites for a witness.

"Honest report" (Acts 6:3)—Philip evidently had a good reputation and was respected by his peers. His life-style was such that he was one of seven deacons chosen from among the Christian community in Jerusalem. A good name is hard to acquire and easily lost. God always forgives a person who is repentant. However, no one can turn back the clock to undo the damage of sin. Let's make sure we walk the walk as we talk the talk. A reputation is much more easily preserved than reconstructed. No one is perfect; but, we must do our best to let our actions speak as loud as our words in witnessing.

"Full of the Spirit" (Acts 6:3,RSV)—the Holy Spirit's work was evident in Philip's life. Every believer has the Holy Spirit, the power of God working in him. We must, like Philip, desire to be filled, that is controlled and empowered, by God's Spirit to the point that we will do his will.

"Full of . . . wisdom" (Acts 6:3)—Wisdom is a God-given (Jas. 1:5) trait that all Christians can have. Philip was respected for having wisdom. Youth may want to dig deeper into the wisdom literature of the Bible, especially Proverbs, and the teachings of James.

"Whom we may appoint over this business" (Acts 6:3)—Philip was being chosen to serve tables (Acts 6:2)! However, his acceptance of this responsibility demonstrates faithfulness, humility, and dedication. All three of these characteristics remind one of Christ! Philip was a servant first, an evangelist later.

Open Minded (Acts 8:5)—Philip's going to Samaria to preach demonstrates his broad-mindedness and willingness to do God's will. The feud between the Jews and Samaritans was centuries old in Philip's day. Jews would generally walk miles out of their way to keep from setting foot on Samaritan soil. In his parable of the good Samaritan, Jesus was shaming his Jewish audience by demonstrating that a Samaritan would do a good thing when Jews would not. Samaritans and Jews had different territories, different places of worship, different customs and above all an ancient hatred that virtually eliminated contact between the two. It is a tribute to Philip's genuine concern for people that the Holy Spirit would choose him to begin breaking down those barriers by taking the good news to Samaritans. In his actions, we have a model to follow. Race, prejudice, or personal feelings cannot interfere with the spread of the gospel.

"Preached Christ" (Acts 8:5)—Philip's subject matter reflected his deep felt sense of concern with what was important. Too often around our unsaved peers we talk about everything else but Christ.

"Arise and go south" (Acts 8:26)—Leadership of God's Spirit is a necessity for a witness.

"And he arose and went" (Acts 8:27)—*Obedience.* In that one word we can see the reason for success in someone like Philip. Obedience is the hallmark of a faithful Christian witness but the downfall of the frustrated follower.

Spirit-filled, full of wisdom, faithful, open-minded. Christ-centered, Spirit-led, and obedient. Such were the qualities presented of Philip, the witnessing deacon. When many youth think of a witnessing Christian, they summon up a vision of some bold, outspoken super salesperson whom they could never imitate. However, youth can and should follow the example of Philip, for he simply did what Christ commanded.

The Ethiopian

God's message to the world was being spread to Jerusalem, Judea, Samaria, and beyond! This was an exciting time for the infant church, as they discovered that God cared about the whole world. Almost daily monumental things were happening to change the disciples' view of the scope of their mission. This man to whom Philip witnessed was important to this "world strategy" as we find out in Acts 8:27.

"Man of Ethiopia"—The ties between this upper valley of the Nile and Jeruslaem go back at least a thousand years to the time of King Solomon and the queen of Sheba. It is known that the area had a substantial Jewish population. Our Ethiopian might have been a natural-born Jew but was more likely a proselyte, one who renounced his pagan heritage to follow the one, true God.

"An eunuch of great authority . . . who had charge of all her treasure"—Today we would probably refer to this official as finance minister or secretary of the treasury. He was obviously a highly placed, important man in the government. "According to the Law, a eunuch could never have any hope of participating fully in the worship of God with the Jews. He could not enter the congregation of Israel (Deut. 23:1)."[1]

"Under Candace the Queen"—Candace was not a proper name but rather a title of a succession of female sovereigns in that country. It is roughly equivalent to *queen*.

This Ethiopian is used as an example of the many nationalities who came to Jerusalem for the feast of Pentecost.

Philip and the Ethiopian Meet

God's plan through the ages has been to redeem humanity. One of life's mysteries is that God uses you and me to accomplish this important plan by telling others of Christ's work. Were our responsibility only some broad nebulous mandate to "say something religious when the time feels right," then our work would be insignificant. However, Jesus continually used specific words: "go," "preach," "you are my witnesses," "Jerusalem." If we follow the Spirit's work in Acts, we see that he gave specific people rather specific assignments: Peter was told to see Cornelius, Ananias was told to see Saul, and in this passage Philip was sent to the Ethiopian. Perhaps today, rather than working to "win the world," we should seek the Holy Spirit's, leadership in a divine appointment with some unsaved person on a day-to-day basis. Such a God-inspired encounter should have these features: preparation by the Spirit, witness of the Word, and demonstration of decision.

That the appointment between Philip and the Ethiopian was prepared by the Spirit can hardly be doubted. The Ethiopian had chosen a desert route rather than traveling the more populated seaside road. Perhaps he wanted to be more secluded to reflect on the things he had heard in Jerusalem. We'll never know all the influences that brought the Ethiopian to a point of decision. Perhaps there were in his own country messianic expectations brought on by Jewish influence. Surely in Jerusalem he had heard of Jesus the Christ and the strange speculations that surrounded him. We might suppose that the Ethiopian was one of the crowd that gathered daily to hear the apostles preach and teach. Whatever the factors used by the Holy Spirit, it was not by accident that the Ethiopian was reading from Isaiah 53 that day, the clearest prophecy in the Old Testament of Christ's mission. This man had reached a place in his life when questions were being asked and answers concerning Christ were needed.

Into this setting stepped God's witness, Philip. Surely Philip had some misgivings about leaving a revival to go into the desert. It's interesting to note that his mission was not identified until he was obedient to God's initial command. Upon arriving at his destination, Philip saw the Ethiopian and was invited to join the caravan. Hearing him read aloud as was the ancient custom, Philip saw an opportunity to be a witness. Notice in Acts 8:30-35 that Philip's witness is based on God's word from Isaiah. Three steps can be seen in the Ethiopian's decision: conviction, understanding, and trust or belief. God's convicting power led to questions; questions led to understanding; understanding led to belief.

A final chapter of this episode can be seen in the Ethiopian's demonstration of his decision. Three evidences may be seen of the Ethiopian's inner decision to trust Christ. First, in Acts 8:37 is a public confession, "I believe that Jesus Christ is the Son of God." The earliest manuscripts omit this verse (see RSV and NASB). However, such a declaration whether recorded here by Luke or not is certainly in order (Rom. 10:9). The second evidence is baptism. Philip must have explained baptism and its importance. Baptism is a direct command of Jesus (Matt. 28:19). Another feature mentioned is the rejoicing of the Ethiopian (Acts 8:39). People react emotionally in different ways and to different degrees. Yet, it cannot be denied that when Jesus enters into people, they are changed for the better. We should expect a difference in a person's life when Jesus enters into it. As a footnote, we can add yet another final evidence. Tradition says that the Ethiopian was named Indich and went back to his country as the first Christian missionary even leading Candace to Christ.

Getting It Together

What then can we learn from Philip and the Ethiopian? Let's look at several concrete applications to our lives.

(1) A Christian witness should have a Christian life-style. It's not recorded that Philip was a witness because of his popularity, good looks, or grades in speech. He was used because of his faithfulness and obedience.

(2) God has appointments for us to keep. Witnessing isn't just handing out tracts on a mission trip. It is a daily, consistent life-style that is characterized by contact with specific people under God's leadership. God will supply the people, the power, and the promises; he simply wants us to be available to be used.

(3) Christian conversion involves a changed life. God's Word takes time

to point out the difference Christ makes. In the accounts of Zacchaeus, the woman at the well, Legion, and the conversion of Saul, among others, specific changes are mentioned in the people's lives. The cycle of witnessing is complete only when the evangelized become the evangelizers.

Youth today can overcome fear of witnessing by learning to depend on God's power and Word.

SUGGESTIONS FOR LEADING THE BIBLE STUDY

From a study of the life of Philip, youth can learn to be effective personal witnesses to the grace of Jesus Christ.

Get Ready

You will need two chenille wires in step 1 for each youth. Write the instructions of the chalkboard. You will need to choose three youth to do the drama in step 2. You will need pencils and paper for step 3. You will also need to prepare your own testimony to give in step 3 if you use the alternate suggestion.

Lead Bible Study

1. As the youth arrive, give each of them two chenille wires. Have the following instructions written on a chalkboard: Create a shape that remind's you of God's love. Be prepared to share what you make and the meaning of the symbol.

(While the youth are working with their chenille wires, help the three youths you chose to prepare the drama called for in step 2.)

When all the youth are finished, have each choose a partner. Ask each youth to share why he chose the shape and how it reminds him of God's love.

2. While most of the youth are working on symbols, arrange a simple dramatization of Acts 8:26-40. Name tags with "angel," "Philip," and "Ethiopian" could be used to indicate the parts. (If you're in a retreat setting, use a sleeping bag pulled by two youth as a "chariot.") The youth can use their own Bibles for the speaking parts. Emphasize that the skit is to be informal, and centered around the biblical account.

When the youth are ready, call on them to present the drama.

3. Prepare a short lecture in which you emphasize why and how Philip witnessed to the Ethiopian. You may also wish to speak to the Ethiopian's question about his being able to participate in Christianity. Then give the results. If you have time, use Philip as an example of a person giving a personal testimony for Jesus.

4. The most common question by youth about witnessing is, What will I

say? Give the youth a pencil and a sheet of paper. Ask them to use the following to write their testimony: "Before I became a Christian," "How I became a Christian," and "Now that I am a Christian." Emphasize that the testimony should be weighted toward the "Now" section, so that the witness can share just how Christ has changed his life. If time permits, encourage the youth to pair off again and share their testimonies with each other. Encourage the youth to put their written testimonies in their Bibles. Later they may refer to their written testimonies when witnessing to another person.

Alternate: You may wish to give your own personal testimony using the above formula, and then ask the youth to write theirs.

Note

1. *Broadman Bible Commentary,* Vol. 10 (Nashville: Broadman Press, 1970), p. 59.

Ruth:

How to Defeat Loneliness

Ruth 1 to 4

Dan G. Kent

Fact Number One: Everyone experiences loneliness.

Oh, yes they do. Everyone does at one time or another, but usually both. When we talk about loneliness, we are talking about something we all face.

Fact Number Two: Something can be done.

Oh, yes it can. We are not helpless. We are not defenseless. There are certain appropriate stances. There are certain appropriate actions. There are responses we can make that will deal with the universal loneliness problem.

Both of these facts are easily proved and demonstrated in the life and Book of Ruth.

The Coming of Loneliness (Ruth 1:1-13)

The Bible gives us an example of someone who dealt effectively with loneliness. Ruth lived before there were kings in Israel, in the time of the judges (1:1). She was an outstanding person. However, like everyone else, she knew tragedy and loneliness.

There was a famine in the land of Israel. A family of four had to leave their home in Bethlehem and relocate in Moab, across the Dead Sea. The parents were Elimelech and Naomi, the sons Mahlon and Chilion (1:1-2).

There was both bad news and good news for this little family. The father died. However, the sons married fine Moabite girls, Orpah and Ruth. Together they enjoyed ten years of happiness before both of the sons also died (1:3-5). (There was a little good news, but clearly there was more bad news).

We are told that losing a mate is the most severe stress anyone can know. A childless widow was an especially unfortunate figure in ancient days. Society made little provision for her, even under the best of circumstances. The Bible mentions such a person in the same breath with the orphan and the foreigner. Widows without children were completely dependent on the thoughtfulness and kindness of their relatives.

Eventually Naomi learned that the famine was over in Israel. She decided it would be best for her to return home. Her daughters-in-law said they would return with her. She tried to talk them out of it. She felt it would be in their best interest to return to their parents' homes. She urged each to return to her mother's tent, as bedouins often did under such circumstances. She wished for each of them a new husband and the security of a happy home (1:6-13).

Both Orpah and Ruth "lifted up their voices and wept" (1:9, NASB). They had lost their husbands. They were about to be parted from Naomi, whom they genuinely cared about. It was a stressful, difficult time for everyone concerned. But Ruth decided to go with Naomi.

Naomi and Ruth moved to Bethlehem. Ruth was a stranger there, even a foreigner, in a new town in a new country. She had no social standing. She was far away from her family and everyone who knew her. Add it all up and it totaled: loneliness.

The Response to Loneliness (Ruth 1:14 to 3:18)

Our type of loneliness may be quite different from what Ruth experienced. However, we know about it too. We may be lonely with acquaintances. We may be lonely in our own homes. We may be lonely in a big crowd at school.

Fortunately, there are things we can do to help our loneliness. We need to pay careful attention to what Ruth did.

Stay close to those who are important (Ruth 1:14-22).—The first thing Ruth did to combat loneliness was to cling to her truest friend. She persisted in her loyalty to Naomi. Orpah went back to her own people (1:14-15), but Ruth refused to do so.

Naomi was not her mother. However, Naomi did care for her. She was important to her. (Naomi became almost a supplementary parent to Ruth, or perhaps even a substitute parent, as Paul did to Timothy and Barnabas did to John Mark.)

The high point of this entire book is in the first chapter. Ruth pledged her love for and loyalty to her mother-in-law, for then and for the rest of her life. She so much as said to Naomi, "Don't try to talk me out of what I intend to do. Don't try to talk me into leaving you. From now on your home, people, God, and tomb will be my own. We will not be separated, either in life or in death" (see 1:16-17).

For Ruth, home was wherever Naomi was. She was determined to go with Naomi, so determined that Naomi gave up trying to talk Ruth out of it (1:18).

The pain of loneliness often makes us act just the opposite of the way Ruth acted. It drives us away from those who are important to us, rather than to them. It drives us away from those who care about us, are really near to us, and want very much to help us. Ruth wouldn't let that happen, and we can't either. She stayed close to Naomi, the one who was so important to her.

Trust in the Lord (Ruth 1:16-17).—Ruth also made a decision about her relationship with the Lord. It, too, was a lifetime and life-changing decision. The last part of 1:16 is what we would call Ruth's profession of faith. She expressed her trust in the Lord.

In 1:16 Ruth used the general name "God," but in 1:17 she used the personal name for God translated "the Lord" in most of our modern versions. It was a special name God revealed to the Hebrew people (Ex. 6:3). It indicates the depth of her commitment to the one true God. She turned away from the idols of her homeland to the one she had evidently learned about and come to know because of her husband and Naomi.

In making this step, Ruth made a choice that changed her life. It changed her life from one of loneliness to one of joy. The change was not immediate. However, it did happen ultimately. It happened eventually. It happened months later, but it did happen.

Ruth's choice also put her in the royal line of David, Israel's greatest hero and king, whose ancestress she became (see 4:13-22). Her choice had a notable impact on the history of the world. The line of David became the genealogy of the new and eternal David, the Messiah (see Matt. 1:5).

"Trust in the Lord" is no rabbit's foot to rub to make loneliness vanish in some magic sort of way. However, it is a necessary part of the proper response to the problem of loneliness.

Stay active (Ruth 2:1-23).—Though she was lonely, Ruth did not sit and sulk. She didn't spend her time feeling sorry for herself, angry at everyone because they weren't solving her problem for her. She couldn't act like that. She had to get out and work. She had to support herself and Naomi. When you are lonely, one of the best things you can do is be active.

Ruth and Naomi arrived in Bethlehem at the beginning of the barley harvest (1:22). Ruth went out to work in the fields. She did so on her own initiative. She suggested it to Naomi (2:2).

Ruth went into the barley fields to glean. She gathered the grain dropped or overlooked by the harvesters (2:3). This was an important way the poor were supported in those days.

Ruth not only worked but also she worked hard, with scarcely a break (2:7). Naomi had a distant relative, Boaz, who owned the field where Ruth worked (2:1-3). When he arrived on the scene, the foreman of the reapers had already noticed Ruth (2:6-7). Boaz insisted that she stay in his fields instead of going somewhere else to glean. He made several provisions for her safety and comfort (2:8,9,14-16).

Ruth had a productive day of work. When evening came, she beat out an ephah of barley, which is estimated at anywhere from a half a bushel to over a bushel. She must have been excited and proud as she showed it to Naomi (2:17-18).

Ruth worked in Boaz' field through the rest of the barley harvest and then through the wheat harvest that started some two to four weeks later (2:23). We could talk a great deal about what a conscientious, unselfish, hardworking person Ruth was. However, for this study the point is that by being active she fought back against the problem of loneliness.

Reach out to others (Ruth 3:1-18).—At this point the pace of the story quickens. At Naomi's suggestion, Ruth took the initiative in personal relationships. She reached out toward one who had shown appreciation for her (2:11) and had indicated a willingness to be her friend.

What Ruth did was alert Boaz to his responsibility as *go'el*. That Hebrew word is usually translated "redeemer" or better still "kinsman redeemer." It refers to a near kinsman who had the responsibility to purchase the property of a dead relative to keep it in the family. He had the responsibility to marry the widow of a deceased relative (like Ruth, the widow of Mahlon), to raise up children in the name of the deceased, to keep his line from dying out. The concept of *go'el* is in the background of much of our biblical understanding of redemption.

Ruth certainly put her best foot forward when she approached Boaz. She washed and anointed herself. She put on her best clothes (3:3). She went to the threshing floor where he and the men were spending the night guarding the valuable crop. She lay down at his feet. Eventually she asked for his protection (3:4,9).

Ruth's actions may seem brash and forward to us today. They were not so back in the time of the judges. What she did may have been standard operating procedure in a place and time thousands of miles away and thousands of years ago.

Besides, Boaz had been kind to her. He was a near relative. He had shown a definite interest in her.

Of course, Boaz agreed to assume the responsibility Ruth suggested to him (3:11). Chapter 4 of the Book of Ruth describes how he did so. Ruth 3:16-18 describes Ruth's report to her mother-in-law. You can sense her excitement as she brought Naomi up to date on what had happened. You can get the feel of their breathless, hurried conversation with its suspense and anticipation.

What if Ruth had stayed in her shell, feeling sorry for herself, angry at the Lord and at others, waiting for someone to reach out to her, waiting for others to make the first move? We don't know how the story would have turned out then, but we do know that because she did what she did, her battle with loneliness had a definitely happy ending (4:13).

SUGGESTIONS FOR LEADING THE BIBLE STUDY

From a study of the life of Ruth, youth can learn about specific resources that will help them deal with loneliness.

Get Ready

You will need pencils and paper for steps 1 and 3. For step 3 you will also need three sheets of newsprint and a felt-tip pen for each work group. For step 2 you will need to prepare the written assignments. You will also need to make an outline of the material in order that you might supplement the report of the youth.

Lead Bible Study

1. Create interest in this study by asking each youth to write:

(1) When was the last time I was truly lonely?

(2) What is the time during my junior and/or senior high years when I remember my most severe bout with loneliness?

Ask the youth to write out the time, place, and circumstances involved in the answers to these two questions. Explain that they need not be shared.

2. Divide the youth into five research groups (or multiples of five if the groups are too large). Distribute these written assignments, asking each team to be prepared to report to the entire class.

Team 1: Write out a brief description of the problem of loneliness in the life of Ruth. Base your description on Ruth 1:4-14,22.

Team 2: Write out a brief description of what Ruth did to combat loneliness, based on Ruth 1:14-22. Emphasize her relationships with other people.

Team 3: Write out a brief description of Ruth's expression of trust in the Lord. Base your description on Ruth 1:16-17. How would this relationship with the Lord aid her in her fight against loneliness?

Team 4: Some people say one way to combat loneliness is to stay active. Write out a brief description of how Ruth used this approach, on Ruth 2:1-7,17.

Team 5: Write out a brief description of Ruth's reaching out to Boaz. Base your description on Ruth 3:1-13.

After ten minutes call for the reports of the research groups. Be ready to supplement the reports based on your own study.

3. Lead youth in the direction of applying this Scripture study by asking

each to list on a sheet of paper the following items. Explain that their responses are for their use only and need not be shared with the group.

(1) The five people who are most important to you. Include family members, church leaders, other adult friends, and friends of your own age. Include only your true friends, those who have stood by you faithfully even during difficult times.

(2) Five activities you enjoy and are involved in or might like to be involved in. Include job, school activities, church activities, service activities, hobbies, and other leisure time activities.

(3) Three people like those on the first list you would like to reach out to, to get to know better, and to become closer to.

Ask the youth to look over each of the three lists they have made and to rank the people and items listed in each category in order of importance. As they finish, point out that they have before them some of their own personal resources like those Ruth used to combat loneliness. Ask them to place their lists in their Bibles or somewhere they can refer to them often.

Divide the youth into three groups (or multiples of three if the groups are too large). Provide a felt-tip pen for each group. Ask each group to write out on newsprint a prayer to the Lord expressing their trust in him as the most special person in their lives. The prayer should describe their relationship with him. It should also indicate their commitment to him and the difference this commitment has made/is making/will make in their lives. The prayer might include an expression of how the youth want the Lord to help them with the problem of loneliness, or a testimony of how he has already done so in times past.

Display the prayers before the class. Ask each group to be ready to share the meanings and motivations behind what they wrote. Ask one youth to close the study session by leading the youth in the praying of one of the prayers displayed.

Samuel:

Learning Effective Citizenship (Fourth of July)

1 Samuel 3:1-21; 8:4-22; 13:4-14; 15:1-35

Dan G. Kent

How many of your youth will be eligible to vote in the next presidential election? Perhaps more than you think. *All* of your youth will be eligible to vote in a presidential election before this decade is over.

Maybe the responsibilities of Christian citizenship will be upon them before they realize it, even before they are ready for it. Maybe we need to study the life of a man like Samuel. He was a man of God, and he often disagreed with his national leaders, but he was loyal to the truest ideals of his nation. A man like that can be a fine model for us today. He can show us ways we can conduct ourselves as effective Christian citizens.

Commit Yourself to the Lord (1 Sam. 3:1-21)

Our nation needs not just citizens, and not just good citizens, but Christian citizens, just as Israel in Samuel's day desperately needed godly citizens. The one who is being the best Christian is being the best citizen. His commitment to the Lord is the most patriotic, most civic thing of all.

We all remember the story of young Samuel, serving old Eli in the shrine at Shiloh. We all know the story of how the Lord called out to Samuel in the night. Samuel mistook the Lord's voice for the call of Eli.

Finally Eli figured out what was happening. He had the maturity and spiritual perception to give Samuel some excellent advice: When you hear the voice again, answer it. "Say, 'Speak, Lord, for Thy servant is listening' " (3:9, NASB).

Samuel followed Eli's instructions. Because he was listening, the Lord was able to reveal his message to and through the young man (3:10-14). It was the beginnng of a life of committed godly living, including committed citizenship.

Samuel's mother, Hannah, gave him to the Lord when he was young (1:24-28). He doubtless learned many important spiritual lessons from her, as well as from his mentor, Eli. He also made the right spiritual choices on his own, such as following Eli's advice in 3:9-10. This is why he grew in the Lord as he did. The Lord was with him. The Lord did not let any of his words fall to the ground. It was not long before everyone in Israel realized that Samuel was a prophet of the Lord (3:19-20).

The first step in proper Christian citizenship is to do what Samuel did. It is to establish a vital, growing relationship with the Lord. It is to emphasize spiritual things. It is to put first things first. It includes leading the upright, godly life Samuel was proud to have led, as admitted by everyone who knew him. When he came to the end of his life, Samuel affirmed that he had not stolen anyone's work animal. He had not defrauded or oppressed anyone. He had taken no bribe (12:3). There was no hint of scandal attaching to his career. No one knew anything that would damage his reputation (12:4-5).

Because of his own strong spiritual base, Samuel was able to lead others in the right spiritual direction. He organized and instructed the "sons of the prophets," groups of young spiritual leaders who preserved the true faith in the Lord during days of difficulty and crisis. He instructed the people and challenged them (12:14-15). He urged wayward people to return to the Lord with all their hearts. He urged them to remove foreign gods so they could serve the Lord alone. He led them in worship services that involved confession of sin and public commitment (7:3-6).

A person with a spiritual commitment, such as Samuel showed, cannot help being more effective as a citizen.

Recognize the Limitations of Government (1 Sam. 8:4-22)

Samuel was a realist, not a naive idealist. He knew what was possible and what was not. He was enough of a student of people, history, and current events to know what was likely to happen and what was not. He also realized that every human institution is less than perfect, as is every human leader.

One of the bitter moments of Samuel's life came when he reached the age of retirement. He was the last and the greatest of the judges, and he hoped that his sons would be able to take his place. It was not to be. His sons didn't measure up to the people's expectations (8:1-3). Instead, the people asked for a king.

Samuel realized the significance of their request. It would mean a complete change in the government of Israel, from the loose tribal league during the time of the judges, to a stronger central government under the kings. (Remember how, in early American history, our country changed from the loose Articles of Confederation to the more tightly organized Constitution?) I have the feeling that the Lord eventually intended to give his people a king anyway, but not so soon.

Samuel didn't like the idea of a monarchy. He didn't like it at all. He turned to the Lord for some instruction. The Lord reassured him and told him to respond to the people's request (8:6-7).

As the Lord directed, Samuel warned the people about the consequences of their decision. He pointed out to them that a monarchy is an imperfect form of government. One reason it is imperfect is that it depends for its administration on imperfect, sinful people, as all forms of government do. The people were evidently well aware of the benefits a new form of government could offer, so Samuel pointed out to them its drawbacks (8:9-18).

The people were not dissuaded. They still wanted a king like the other nations had, a king who could judge them and lead them into battle. So the Lord—and Samuel—agreed.

Sometimes we think that the form of government we grew up under and are most familiar with is automatically the best in the world. And it may be—democracy certainly has good arguments in its favor. However, sometimes we go even beyond a position like that: We act as if a form of government is perfect, the best it could possible be. This is never true. No human leader and no human institution is without fault. (Winston Churchill is supposed to have called democracy the worst form of government, except for all others that have ever been tried.)

It is a mistake for us to accept without reservation a political leader, political party, or party platform. No person is all right without any wrong. No group or agenda is always right, never wrong. Every form of government can be improved. It can be made more honest, equitable, and just—and Christians are obligated to help make it so. Even so great a nation as our own can be better than it is. That is where we as citizens who believe in Jesus Christ come in.

Put the Truth First (1 Sam. 13:4-14; 15:1-35)

Samuel was loyal, both to his nation of Israel and to the king he himself had anointed. He was a true patriot. However, he did not make his country or any political leader a god. He did not become idolatrous in his patriotism.

A true citizen puts the lord first, not his nation. He puts the truth first, instead of any lesser value. He puts the Lord's will first. If his nation or its leaders do not also do that, he lovingly and loyally works to correct what cannot help but become a worse situation.

First Samuel 13 tells of how King Saul prepared to do battle with Israel's enemies of long-standing, the Philistines. It promised to be a crucial and decisive battle (13:5). Saul was anxious about the outcome and anxious to move to the attack before the enemy became better prepared.

But Israel generally saw her engagements as wars in the name of the

Lord. The troops were not so much national warriors as servants of the Lord. They were holy to the Lord. They fought in his name. They fought with his help and according to his direction. Often the spoils of battle were also his.

This is why Saul and the troops waited at Gilgal for the aging Samuel to appear, bless the troops, and offer sacrifice (13:8). The only problem was that Samuel didn't appear. Evidently, as you get older, you also get more independent. Samuel seems to have decided it wouldn't hurt them to wait on him a little while.

The king grew more and more impatient. He began to notice an impatience on the part of the troops. He worried that his army might begin to break up (13:7-8). Finally he took matters into his own hands. He impulsively decided that he would act the part of the priest and offer the sacrifice himself (13:9), even though such audacity was strictly forbidden.

Wouldn't you know it? As soon as he finished, Samuel walked up. Saul, as always, had his excuses ready. The army was scattering, and Samuel was late, and the Philistines were coming (13:11).

Samuel rebuked his king. He said Saul had acted foolishly. He had not kept the commandment of the Lord. His rash disobedience would have dire consequences in the future. His kingdom would not endure. Instead the Lord would give it to another, more worthy man (13:13-14).

Almost the same thing happened later when the Lord sent Saul to be his instrument of judgment against the sinful Amalekites (15:2-3). Saul defeated them easily. However, once again he decided that his way was better than the Lord's way. Once again he disobeyed. He spared the king and the choice animals (15:7-9).

Of course, Saul claimed he was obedient (15:13), but Samuel confronted him with the evidence of his turning away from following the Lord (15:14). Again Saul began to make excuses. *The people* were the ones who spared all the fat, show animals. They did it to offer nice sacrifices to the Lord (15:15,21). That was when Samuel said that the Lord wants obedience, not sacrifice: "To obey is better than sacrifice" (15:22, NASB). The Lord would rather we do what he wants us to than to later say we are sorry. Disobedience is the same type of sin as idolatry (15:23).

In Old Testament times, a prophet was one who revealed the Lord's will for his people. He fearlessly announced the truth to them. Samuel was a true prophet. He put truth first, even ahead of country. He put principles first. He put the Lord and his will first. This is why he was such a great citizen, able to help make his country great.

A man is famous in American history for saying something like "My country, right or wrong." Samuel never said anything like that. He knew that no nation needs "yes men" who will agree automatically with whatever is done. Instead a nation needs people who will continue to care (15:35) and who will use all their power to keep their country pointed toward what is right.

SUGGESTIONS FOR LEADING THE BIBLE STUDY

From a study of the life of Samuel, youth can learn to commit themselves to engage in an expression of effective citizenship.

Get Ready

Set up a registration table or booth for step 1. Also prepare the lecture. For step 2 prepare the written assignments for the work groups. Gather material for group 2. You will need a chalkboard and chalk for step 3.

Lead Bible Study

1. Create interest in the Bible study by setting up beforehand a table or booth labeled: Voter Registration. Ask the youth to stand who will be eligible to vote in the next presidential election. Allow a few moments for them to determine this. Then ask the other youth to stand who will be eligible to vote in a presidential election in this decade.

Point out that the responsibilities of Christian citizenship will be upon them before they realize it, perhaps before they are ready for it. Give a brief lecture to explain how the study of the life of Samuel will help prepare for citizenship responsibilities.

2. Lead the youth to examine the Scripture passages for themselves. Organizing the youth into three work groups (or multiples of three if the groups are large). Distribute the following written assignments.

(1) Ask group 1 to write a diary of spiritual growth for Samuel. Write the diary like you would write a diary for yourself. Base your work on 1 Smauel 3:1-21 (Samuel's response to God's call); 1 Samuel 7:3-6 (Samuel's decision and challenge to serve God only); 1 Samuel 12:3-5 (Samuel's refusal to use his office for personal gain at the expense of the people). Be ready to report to the entire class.

(2) Use a felt-tip pen to list on newsprint the strengths and weaknesses (advantages and disadvantages) of the form of government Israel was discarding (the loose tribal confederation of the judges) and the form of government Israel was adopting (monarch), including the strengths and weaknesses of the leaders in each case. (Give this group the background material in this lesson, other resources on this period of history, and 1 Sam. 8:4-22.) If you have time, complete the same activity for democracy and our country's leaders.

(3) Write out a description of: the mistakes Saul made in 1 Samuel

13:4-14; 15:1-35; the reasons he made these mistakes; the excuses Saul gave, and what Samuel said about Saul and his actions. Be ready to report to the entire class.

Call for reports. Be ready to supplement the reports based on your own study. Be ready in particular to show how each report relates to the Bible study statement under "Suggestions for Leading the Bible Study."

3. Help the youth to apply the truth of the Scriptures passages to their lives by asking them to name things they will be able to do to help America during this decade. List these on a chalkboard. You and other leaders should be prepared to make additional suggestions.

Ask each youth to silently adopt one of these activities and write it down so he may keep it permanently. Allow several volunteers to lead in sentence prayers for the Lord's help as each tries to carry out the activity chosen.

Timothy:

Accepting Responsibility

Acts 16:1-3; 1 Timothy 4:11-16; 2 Timothy 1:5

B. J. Dean

Have you ever identified a person by saying, "Oh, you know Sam. He's always with Jack." Sam could be a perfectly nice, capable person, but he will probably always be known because of his association with Jack. This study deals with a well-known minor character in the Bible who was like Sam. It has been said that Timothy might "never have been remembered had he not crossed the path of a man whom the world can never forget." In the New Testament, Timothy is mentioned twenty-four times and all but one of those was because of his association with Paul.

Meet the Young Man (Acts 16:1-3; 2 Tim. 1:5)

What do we know about Timothy, the man? Not a great deal, but let's examine the facts we have.

Timothy lived in a small town of Lystra located on the major commercial road from Antioch into Syria. His mother was a Jewess, and his father was a Greek. Apparently Timothy's Gentile father had allowed his wife, Eunice, to bring their son up in the Jewish faith but had drawn the line at circumcision, refusing to allow what the Greeks considered a kind of branding. The time of the father's death is not known, but it may have been early in Timothy's life. Neither do we know when Eunice was converted to Christianity. But sometime before the development of their relationship with the apostle Paul, both his grandmother Lois and the young Timothy also became believers. It would seem that Timothy had been reared in a home where his religious development was given careful attention. He was brought up thinking about other people and living in such a way that godly conduct was natural to him (Phil. 2:19-20).

We know nothing about Timothy's conversion. Most of his life he had been aware of the ways of the Lord. Timothy responded with a faith of his own and with a commitment to vocational Christian service.

When Paul met him at Lystra, Timothy was already well-thought-of by the Christian community there. Paul and Barnabas had disagreed over John Mark accompanying them on a second missionary journey and had parted company. Paul decided to take Silas with him, and he wanted a third member on the team. He chose Timothy. Because it was important for Timothy to be accepted by the Jewish communities, Paul deemed it necessary for Timothy to be circumcised.

Paul often called Timothy his son in the spirit. This must have been a source of joy to both of them, and each gained from their relationship.

Growing Up the Hard Way

For approximately five years, Timothy spent most of his time in Paul's company. Can you imagine what a thrill this must have been for a young preacher? During this time Timothy had traveled with Paul and Silas and had gone to Thessalonica alone on a mission for Paul. Timothy was learning, but he still had not learned all that he needed to know. Paul then assigned Timothy a task beyond the young man's capabilities.

Grave problems had arisen in the church at Corinth. The difficulties were of moral, doctrinal, and administrative natures. Paul sent first a letter to the church, urging the Christians to give a good reception to Timothy (1 Cor. 4:17; 16:10-11). Unfortunately Timothy was not successful in this assignment. Why? Not because he lacked abilities, not because he lacked experience, but because he was too young. The church was hostile because Paul had not come himself (1 Cor. 4:18-19), and they did not accept this young substitute. With these feelings against him, Timothy did not accomplish his task. But failure is not a disgrace, and Paul never held this against Timothy. Actually, it may be more accurate to say that Timothy did not succeed, but he was not a failure.

But He's So Young (1 Tim. 4:11-12)

The nominating committee in your church has two possible teachers for a class of median adults. Both are qualified; one is about the same age or a little older, and the other is several years younger than the class members. Which one do you think will be given the teaching position? Probably the older—and that may seem a bit unfair. Is there a way to change the seemingly common idea that an older person is more believable simply because he is older? Paul seemed to think so, and he wanted Timothy to combat that concept.

There were problems in the church at Ephesus, and Paul left Timothy there to try and improve the situation. He felt that Timothy, though young, was qualified for the responsibility. He wrote the young preacher the letter we know as 1 Timothy, giving him instructions about the care of this congregation until Paul could return.

First Paul wanted Timothy to stop being timid and to start being firm. Then he wanted Timothy to be an example in everything he did and said. Paul continued to consider himself Timothy's spiritual father (1 Tim. 1:2) and at times spoke to Timothy as if he were a child. In 1 Timothy 4:11, Paul used that tone. Paul told Timothy to command and teach those things he had written to the Christians at Ephesus. Command? How is a command different? It comes with the sound of authority that says, "I am qualified and authorized to command. Listen to me and do what I say!" From a young Christian to older ones? Yes, if the younger one can demonstrate that he is worthy of respect and obedience. Paul continued by giving Timothy more advice that would give the young preacher the support of his congregation. Read again 1 Timothy 4:12.

Youth should not be a handicap. Actually youth is a relative factor. To an eighty-year-old man a sixty-year-old is young. When he received his assignment at Ephesus, Timothy was at least in his thirties. By the standards of the youth with whom you work, Timothy was not really young. But like some of them might try to do, it is possible that Timothy had used as an excuse for his failure to behave responsibly, "I am too young!" Paul wanted Timothy to know that such reasoning was not acceptable.

Paul said in effect, "If you don't want to be criticized, act in such a way that you are above criticism." One's actions are to be determined by love, faith, loyalty, and purity. If Timothy—or any believer —should behave in such a manner, it will become evident that, in the Christian experience, authority comes from what one is rather than from how long he has lived. Stated another way, words and arguments will not stop criticism; conduct will.

What kind of love was Timothy to show? The kind of love that comes from the head as well as the heart. In other words the Christian leader chooses to love people regardless of how they may treat him. It is an act of will.

What kind of loyalty was he to show? A faithfulness to Christ that did not count the cost was needed. It is not always easy to be faithful to one's beliefs. For the Christian leader, however, it is the way he chooses to live.

What kind of purity? A never-failing allegiance to the standards of Christ was required. The mark of a Christian leader is his choice to live by those standards of his Savior rather than by the standards of the world.

"In word, in conversation" had to do with Timothy's public life, while the others related to his private life. It is important to understand that the way one acts/reacts in public reflects what one is in private.

Live the Lesson (1 Tim. 4:13-16)

In the interim before Paul's arrival, Timothy was to occupy himself with three pursuits relating to Christian worship: reading and preaching the word, instruction in the great truths of the faith, and finally in the Christian actions that always follows real worship.

Timothy—like every Christian—had a special gift that he was not to neglect. A gift left undeveloped would/will be lost. Nurture such a gift by practicing or meditating on that gift until the using of it becomes second nature. The next instruction was for Timothy to keep a careful eye on himself and on his teachings. What he did and what he said had to be in agreement. They still do.

Timothy was urged to progress so that his growth would be evident to all. Many of us spin our wheels in the same old ruts. We content ourselves with a limited number of favorite ideas. New ideas, new concepts that seek to set our faith in contemporary terms are a threat. This should not be true in the lives of Christians and especially in the lives of Christian leaders. The Christian thinker should strive always to be an adventurous thinker.

Paul told Timothy that he was to continue in his spiritual growth. Each year we should be more Christlike than we were the year before. Our task is to lead others to Christ. If we are not growing, our witness will lack strength.

And So . . .

From Timothy we learn that (1) it is no disgrace to fail so long as one does not accept failure as a life-style; (2) being a Christian involves responsibility at every age; (3) one's words and actions reflect one's relationship to Christ at any age; (4) worship is a vital part of Christian growth at every age.

SUGGESTIONS FOR LEADING THE BIBLE STUDY

From a study of the life of Timothy youth can recognize reasons for and ways to accept responsibility.

Getting Ready

Prepare a focal wall using large, colorful letters to spell out Timothy: Accepting Responsibility.

Duplicate the work sheets needed for step 1.

Place a sheet of newsprint labeled *Timothy—the Man* on the wall for the brainstorming in step 2.

Prepare the chart described in step 4.

Put the "And So" statements on a sheet of newsprint to use in step 5.

Lead Bible Study

1. Distribute to each youth a copy of the work sheet with the following statements on it.

1. I'll be glad when I am old enough to . . .
2. My parents think I am too young to . . .
3. but old enough to . . .
4. My church thinks I am too young to . . .

5. but old enough to . . .

6. I think the best age to be is . . .

7. Right now the biggest problem with being my age is . . .

8. The hardest thing about being a teenager is . . .

9. A biblical youth I can identify with is . . .

10. When Paul told Timothy "Let no man despise thy youth," I think Timothy must have been . . .

After allowing time for the youth to complete the sheets, ask them to form triads to share their responses. Then share some from each triad with the large group ending with statement 10.

2. On a large sheet of newsprint list some facts that the youth know about Timothy that are discovered through a brainstorming session. Using these and the background section on "Meet the Young Man," present a lecture on the personal background of Timothy.

3. Ask the youth to distinguish between "failing" and "being a failure." (The first is an occurrence and the second is a life-style.) Explain Timothy's experience at the church at Corinth and Paul's response to that happening.

4. Put up a sheet of butcher paper labeled as follows:

COMMAND

Love	In word/conversation
Faith	
Loyalty	In Private
Purity	

After instructing the youth to listen for information about the words/phrases on the chart, enlist a youth to read aloud 1 Timothy 4:11-16. From the background sections "But He's So Young" and "Live the Lesson," present a lecture/discussion that will explain the chart. Add these explanations to the visual.

5. Put the "And So" statements on the focal wall and allow the youth to respond to each. State that one cannot excuse irresponsible conduct because of age but that one can use one's age to progress in acting responsibly. Refer again to the work sheet used in step 1 and ask the youth to consider again numbers 7 and 1 and share their ideas about how the instructions Paul gave to Timothy can be related to these statements.

Remind the youth that age is relative and that being young is a condition that is cured with time! Close with a prayer that God will help each person present realize that age is not an excuse for wrong doing but a challenge to grow and develop a positive life-style of Christian living.

Zacchaeus:

Money or God

Luke 19:1-10

Forrest W. Jackson

The following is an account of Luke 19:1-10 as it might have occurred between a Reporter for the *Jerusalem News* and Zacchaeus. The reporter has set up an interview with Zacchaeus in his home in Jericho.

REPORTER: Zacchaeus, we have received word that you have given away about $500,000 in the last few months. Is there any truth to that story?

ZACCHAEUS: Yes, it is true. But how did you find out? I certainly didn't advertise my giving.

REPORTER: Well, it's pretty hard to keep $500,000 quiet! A new orphanage in Jericho, a new senior citizens' home, new bank accounts for former clients, and handouts to people too numerous for me to keep an account, that's a lot of money on the move.

ZACCHAEUS: It does sound pretty crazy, doesn't it? Why would anyone in his right mind give half of his savings account to the poor?

REPORTER: That's a good question, all right. I would love to hear the answer.

ZACCHAEUS: Well you had better sit down. It will take awhile for me to tell the story. (*Pause.*) You know, of course, that I am the chief tax collector of the Jericho area. (*Reporter nods.*) I had to pay a large sum of money to get that job. And I had to hire several people to help me collect the taxes in this large area. So it cost me a lot of money just to get started.

At first, I collected only a reasonable fee. I had to get back my cost, plus make a little money. However, no one appreciated my fairness. The people called me a traitor to my country. They called me a common thief. My name was constantly linked with prostitutes and Gentiles. I can't tell you how mad that made me. So I said, "OK, if that's the way you want it, two can play that game." I put the word out that the tax would be doubled. One-half for the Romans and one-half for me. I became a very rich man. I became obsessed with money. I decided to become as rich as old Herod himself.

REPORTER: I can see by your house that money is no object for you.

ZACCHAEUS: I soon found that money was not everything. In fact, I found that it cannot buy the things a person really desires: love, friends, and real fellowship. I was rich, but I was lonely and miserable. I guess it was the loneliness that first caused me to look for something better. But I couldn't find it in the religion of my people. To the religious leaders, I was an outcast.

REPORTER: Why was that?

ZACCHAEUS: They said I wasn't fit to worship. I wasn't welcome in the Temple. I was treated as though God didn't approve of me. I guess I believed it! That's why it became so easy for me to bleed my own people with high taxes. I just acted like the person they said I was. But then I began to hear about a person who accepted prostitutes, tax collectors, Gentiles, and all kinds of people.

REPORTER: You mean Jesus of Nazareth?

ZACCHAEUS: Yes. I had never met him. But the stories I heard were really something. He was different from the Jewish religious leaders. He had fellowship with people who were outcasts. It was told that Jesus accepted people as they were and forgave their sins. I became intrigued by his reputation. I wanted very much to meet him. Of course, I couldn't leave my tax collectors long enough to do that. They would have stolen me blind. You know, money does that to you. You get where you'll do anything to get money. Then one day while I was in the courtyard of my home, I overheard someone say that Jesus was coming through Jericho on his way to Jerusalem. I felt that I *must* see him.

REPORTER: You sound as though it was a problem for you.

ZACCHAEUS: It was. First, I look like I'm sitting down when I'm standing up. Second, the streets were lined with people. When I tried to get through, they tightened up, shoved me, and called me names.

REPORTER: What did you do?

ZACCHAEUS: I kept going down the line of people until I found an opening. I could tell the people would keep moving along and pushing me out of the way. They really enjoyed pushing me. Also I could tell by the noise that Jesus was getting nearer. I moved a little farther to a point where there was a sycamore tree. The sycamore tree has branches low enough that even I could climb it. So I climbed into the tree and hoped no one would bother me.

REPORTER: What did you think of this Jesus when he passed by?

ZACCHAEUS: That's just it! He stopped right under me and called me by my name. I nearly fell on top of him. When I finally got down, I asked, "What did you say?" Jesus said, "I must stay at your house today" (Luke 19:5, TEV). I was so tickled that I just stood there grinning like a fool. When I finally could speak, I embarrassed myself. I said, "Oh please be my guest! It has been so long since anyone came to see me. I would love to have you spend the night before you go on to Jerusalem."

REPORTER: And did all that mob follow you and Jesus to your house?

ZACCHAEUS: Not on your life! As soon as Jesus said he was going to be my guest, the crowd broke into a shocked murmuring. They sounded like a hot sports car with unleaded gas whose valves are protesting the lack of octane. The only people who followed Jesus were the apostles. Everyone else left Jesus cold. I suspect that even some of the apostles were uptight at the change in the mood of the people.

REPORTER: How did this affect Jesus?

ZACCHAEUS: I couldn't tell that it affected him at all. He gave his full attention to me. It was as though he had come to Jericho just to see me. We had a great time. My servants prepared a meal fit for a king. You ought to see that fellow named Peter eat! And Matthew took care of his part of the food also. He had been a tax collector before following Jesus. But Jesus spent so much time reassuring me of his acceptance, he didn't eat much. However, he sure did feed me, if you know what I mean.

REPORTER: I'm not sure I follow you.

ZACCHAEUS: Well, as Jesus and I reclined at the table, his presence and words convicted me of my sin. I realized that, even though I was a son of Abraham, I was worshiping the god of materialism. I also knew that the rejection and isolation given me by the people was no excuse for robbing them the way I had done. I felt a little sick. I knew I had to make a decision. And I did.

I got up from the table and spoke directly to Jesus. I said, "Listen, sir! I will give half my belongings to the poor, and if I have cheated anyone, I will pay him back four times as much" (v. 8, TEV).

Then Jesus said to me, "Salvation has come to this house today, for this man, also, is a descendant of Abraham" (v. 9, TEV). In that moment, I felt as though a heavy burden had been lifted from my shoulders. I felt right with the world. And I was no longer controlled by a love for money nor the desire for revenge against my people. Since that day, I have been a changed man. Now I know what Jesus meant when he said, "The Son of Man came to seek and to save the lost" (v. 10, TEV). Oh yes, my entire family has followed me in becoming disciples of Jesus.

REPORTER: I must say I am very impressed. However, I'm not sure what my editor will say when I turn in this story. I doubt that he will know what to do with a story telling that Jesus saves the lost.

Some Biblical Notes on Luke 19:1-10

19:1 **Jericho:** Located not far from the Jordan River within the border of Judea about fifteen miles northeast of Jerusalem. It was the winter capital of the Herods.

19:2 **Zacchaeus:** The name means pure.

Chief tax collector: This term is not used elsewhere and its exact significance is not known. It probably means a person with other tax collectors working under him. Tax collectors were generally classified with prostitutes, robbers, and Gentiles. They were considered traitors to their country.

19:3 **On account of the crowd:** Apart from being a short person, the crowd probably delighted in keeping him back. They would enjoy pushing, shoving, and bruising him.

19:4 **Sycamore tree:** Sometimes called a fig mulberry and sometimes called a sycamore fig. This tree had a fruit similar to a fig tree. Its fruit was eaten by the poor.

19:6 **Received him joyfully:** The Gospels often show people who were called "sinners" receiving Jesus with joy while the "religious" people often rejected him.

19:7 **Guest . . . of a sinner:** Someone has said, "How odd of God to choose the Jews!" Yes. And to choose Zacchaeus! And you! Verse 10 explains verse 7.

19:8 **Stood:**Zacchaeus was probably reclining at the table with Jesus. Standing would claim everyone's attention for Zacchaeus' testimony.

Half of my goods . . . restore it fourfold: This shows how radical Zacchaeus had changed. He now served a God who called for ethical and moral living. Giving "half" may have been hyperbole, but it expressed the new direction of his life. This was far beyond what might have been expected.

19:9 **Salvation:** The change in Zacchaeus was seen in his actions. Caring for the poor has always been acceptable to God. Zacchaeus had become one of the "doers of the word" (Jas. 1:22, RSV).
Salvation had come to Zacchaeus' house in the person of Jesus Christ.

Son of Abraham: This meant that Zacchaeus was one of God's chosen people. He was a person for whom Jesus was about to die. Zacchaeus was worthy of salvation, as much as any other human being.

19:10 This verse shows that Jesus came to save all people, since all are "lost." Jesus excludes no one, except those who exclude themselves by unbelief.

SUGGESTIONS FOR LEADING BIBLE STUDY

From a study of the life of Zacchaeus, youth can learn that God is more important than money.

Get Ready

1. Enlist two youth to do the parts of Zacchaeus and the reporter. It is the type of material that could be read. It would help if the youth, especially the

one portraying Zacchaeus, became familiar with their parts. Choose youth who can give the parts a little zest.

2. Prepare listening sheets for the other youth to fill in while listening to the interview. The following could be used.

(1) What did it mean that Zacchaeus was a "chief tax collector"? _____

_____

(2) What did the people think of tax collectors? _____

_____

(3) Why do you think Zacchaeus wanted to see Jesus? _____

_____

(4) How did Zacchaeus respond to Jesus' request to go home with him? _____

_____

(5) How did the crowd respond to Jesus' going home with Zacchaeus? _____

_____

(6) What do you think Jesus and Zacchaeus talked about at the table? _____

_____

(7) Why did Zacchaeus say he would give half of his living to the poor and repay any theft four times? _____

_____

(8) What did Jesus mean when he said, "Salvation has come to this house today" (v. 9)? _____

(9) What does it mean to you personally that Jesus "came to seek and save the lost" (v. 10)? _____

_____

3. Read through the interview and fill out one of the sheets yourself. This will help you prepare to lead the discussion of the youth's answers.

4. Prepare assignment cards for the four groups.

Lead Bible Study

1. Give each youth a listening sheet and a pencil. Tell them that they will observe an interview and fill in their listening sheets from what they observe. Ask the two youth enlisted to give the interview of the reporter and Zacchaeus to do so.

If you do not have two youth who would enjoy reading the drama, consider having two people record the drama and play it for your youth.

2. When the two youth have finished, thank them for their presentation. They may join you to help lead the discussion, if you choose. Take the questions one by one. Ask youth to respond by sharing their answers. You may add your own insights. Allow for diversity of opinion.

3. Ask the youth to open their Bibles to Luke 19:1-10. Ask them to read the account and compare the attitude of Jesus toward Zacchaeus to the attitude of the crowd toward Zacchaeus. Give the youth pencil and paper. Instruct them to write a paragraph comparing and contrasting the two attitudes. Allow about ten minutes for this work. Ask several of the youth to share their paragraph.

4. Divide the youth into several groups, not more than five to a group. Give the following assignments (double up if your group is large). Group 1: What was Zacchaeus' relation to money *before* he met Jesus? Be prepared to use Luke 19:1-10 to support your answer. Group 2: What was Zacchaeus' relation to money *after* he met Jesus? Be prepared to use Luke 10:1-10 to support your answer. Group 3: What was Jesus' attitude toward Zacchaeus who obviously had gotten rich by misusing people? Be prepared to use Luke 19:1-10 to support your answer. Group 4: Using Luke 19:1-10 to support your answer, how does Jesus want us to be related to money? Allow about ten minutes for the group to get their reports together. Call for reports.

5. Close the session by following up on the report of Group 4. You may wish to add to the report if the youth did not make clear that Jesus expects us to use money to help others. Jesus expects us to make money honestly without taking advantage of others. In short we are to control our money. Our money should not control us.

Ask, What are some things you can do this week to have the attitude of Jesus toward money? (Included might be: don't take advantage of the poor, use personal income to help someone in need, don't make money in sinful ways, extend Christian love to those who take financial advantage of you, and others.)

Call on someone, or lead in prayer yourself, to pray for God to give each person the courage to do what God would have him to do.